The Pyramid of Rational Thought and How It Leads to Extinction

Carl Nelson

ISBN:0692655522
ISBN-13:9780692655528

DEDICATION

To my wife Lynn and son Tin Tin with all my love and best arguments.

Look for all these books on the Magic Bean label.

Magic Bean Books

Plays by Carl Nelson:
Into the Wild Blue Yonder
Personal Growth Through Copier Sales
Ollie's Day Out

Essays by Carl Nelson:
The Audience is a Mob
The Pyramid of Rational Thought and How It Leads to Extinction

Poetry by Carl Nelson:
A Poet's Past Lives
Shoving My Way Into the Conversation
I'm Forgetting Things in My Dreams

Fiction by Eldon Cene
Murders In Progress
The Cognitive Web
The Mind Wars

All are currently available through Amazon books.
&
http://www.magicbeanbooks.co/home.html

Cover drawing by Tin Tin Nelson. Used with permission.

CONTENTS

ACKNOWLEDGMENTS

I would like to thank all of the people at Magic Bean Books who have made this publication possible. Nothing seems beyond their skill set.

This was my first post:

Hello world!
March 9, 2010

A lot of fertility; very little form. Here we go...

Leaf through, pick an entry, enjoy a skein of thought unrolling.

THE PYRAMID OF RATIONAL THOUGHT AND HOW IT LEADS TO EXTINCTION

My rational, highly-educated, scientifically minded, progressive friends who apparently care more about people that I do, believe that the world would be a better place and our lives would be happier if run on a more 'rational' base.

They are exerting every method of persuasion in their toolbox, from ridicule to downright contempt, to 'reason' us out of our irrational compulsions for religion, tradition, hard work, rule of law, private ownership, or whatever asinine thing the poor benighted masses and others 'of my ilk' might think of next, like enjoying a Big Mac with bacon and cheese. But study this diagram:

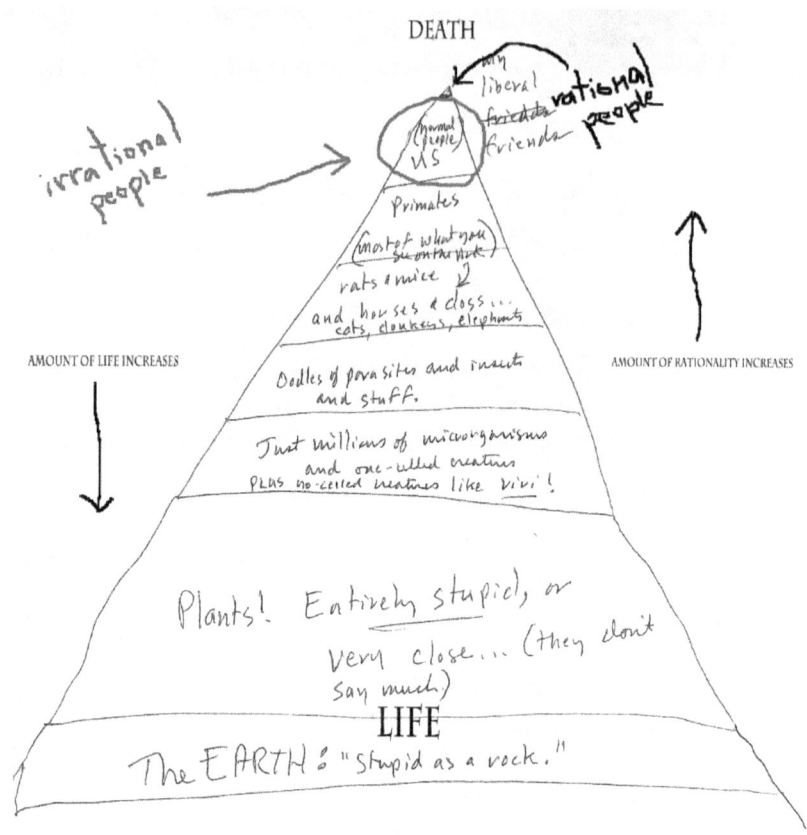

The Pyramid of Rational Thought

The facts of these matters seem to say otherwise. Study this **Pyramid of Life** (above).

We see that the greater the intelligence of the species, the smaller its population. This is true for every species you might say, *except for humans*. Humans seem to be the exception, multiplying at a crazy pace, and ever threatening the planet's carrying capacity.

How do we do this?

My rational friends would say that of course, we *aren't* doing this; that we are, in fact, headed for extinction, or a grand apocalypse. And their rational explanations end in a doomsday analysis, from planetary depletion of resources, to fouling of the ecosystem, to global warming, to simple global self-immolation... and on and on. And that it's crazy and irrational to think otherwise.

However, a rational person would also have to note that these folks have been making these doomsday predictions for quite some time. Malthus, the great vertebra of the doomsday scenario, published his Essay on the Principle of Population in 1798, and rational thinkers have been predicting a Malthusian catastrophe ever since. In my youthful years it was Paul Ehrlich who took up the banner. He's pretty passé currently and there are lots more youthful Cassandras out there now. You won't have any trouble locating them.

These people are always finding meaning in nature - picking it apart with their rational tweezers - and well they should. Nature is very rational. Everything out there is running around for good reason. And the more intelligent the plants and animals have become, the more they begin running about for very, very good reasons... never wasting their resources. Until, if you extend the side of the pyramid upwards – there is no one left... and for some very, good reason. And what is this reason?

My own theory is that *rational thought, when tied too tightly to a higher intelligence, is a good recipe for extinction.* Study the pyramid.

I contend that we *are* crazy. As a species we are highly irrational. Which is what saves us from extinction. *It is our craziness, as a species, which allows us to produce the unforeseeable – and not our reason.* Our reason produces only the foreseeable. Reason can only extend. And then, reason can only age. And then, it can only die. (An interesting associated speculation would be whether this diminishes the theoretical threat and/or long range viability of Artificial Intelligence?)

At one time, imagining the earth as round was thought of as crazy. Sailing off the edge of the world was surely a crazy undertaking. Baboons don't do it. Why go to the moon? Dogs don't do it. Why fly? Why look into a microscope? You ever see a chicken wasting its time doing that? Why count the stars? Why put bananas on your peanut butter sandwich? Why not kill people and take what they have? Why waste your time worshipping? Why read fiction? It seems a good bet that it is our craziness which has expanded the carrying capacity of our predicament and allowed us to flourish to this unprecedented state.

We're all crazy. (And especially all these informed, rational people.) *Respect this.* That's how we stay alive.

Diagram by Carl Nelson – no rights reserved :)

YOUR AUTHOR BECOMES A PSYCHONAUT

Both my son, and wife and a couple friends thought this was nuts, but there are a couple things I've wanted to try out. One is wearing a Ghillie suit.

The other is trying an *isolation tank*. So when the wife and son left for Ohio this week, I got my chance to visit the float/sensory deprivation chamber experience outlet in the Greenlake area. http://floatseattle.com/ Their website says, "overcome: stress" "conquer: fear" "achieve: theta state". I wasn't looking to accomplish any of these. But, hey! They all seem like good things.

What concerned me most going into this was first, whether I could get back out. I wanted to be sure this 'isolation tank' had an internal latch. My second worry was whether I'd be slipping into some greasy slurry formerly inhabited by lots of other sweaty, hairy, poorly bathed isolationists. My third worry was if I'd have to do this naked? A fourth worry was that if I fell asleep, would I drown?

Well, "Float Seattle" is a new, modern, well designed facility. The tanks are flushed after each use and the Epsom salt plus Bromine in water solution is filtered and then reused. The door has no latch. And everyone gets a private, fairly spacious room with a shower. The 'tank' was tall enough to stand up in and had a blue interior light which could be turned on and off. They give you earplugs to dampen any conducted sound and also to keep the solution out. And a slightly synthetic Jamaican/African bongo/percussion beat, which comes and goes and starts softly, reminds you when your time is up. Yeah, and you immerse naked.

Judging from the half dozen, or more, customers which I saw, Float Seattle attracts fairly attractive, younger to middle aged introverted sorts who 'dwell in their body' more than others. Not the extroverted competitive types nor the hairy wilderness trekkers, but more the urban yoga types who watch their diets and weight and are proud of their posture and flexibility. I stuck out a bit as I was much taller, much older, had a paunch, and am about as flexible as a rusted gate – though I *am* introverted.

I'd imagined the tank solution coming up to my knees, but in fact it was only around 10 inches deep. The temperature is controlled so that you neither sweat nor chill while immersed, which for my temperament makes it a little warm for inducing sleep. The most interesting part of my time in the tank was the experience of buoyancy. The solution makes you so buoyant that you needn't a headrest; your head floats naturally and comfortably. And you needn't fight to stay afloat. The feeling is of lying on a soft slippery neoprene surface (or 'hand') which 'lifts', exerting the same pressure everywhere. We all know the 'feel' of water when we are being the active force. But when the water holds us up – 'pushes back' – the feel is quite different, very slick, very alien. It feels like 100 percent humidity with the body fluids pushing in instead of leaking out. It was a very odd feeling, but enjoyable. And my one regret is that I didn't spend more time trying different postures and playing in the solution.

Instead I rested entirely motionless. I wanted to find out if an absolute lack of sensory information would tend me towards psychosis or even nudge me a couple psychocentimeters towards an internal chaos. Nope. Instead, the only mental sensation I had which I seemed *pretty sure of* was boredom. My thoughts did not race. Repressed emotions and past memories did not overwhelm me. In fact, I found it very tedious to think at all. If I had indeed achieved a theta state and was truly 'inhabiting' my body, then mentally it felt a lot like waiting in a car, in silence at the grocery store.

And here I can't say if my reaction is normal, or if my particular nature is so off the charts as to completely invalidate the experience. But frankly, being in my body is not something I particularly relish. And probably many others do. I generally think of my body as I think of my car. I want my body to take me where I want to go, be reliable, be low maintenance, and not embarrass me in front of others. But I enjoy 'being in my body' about as much as I would enjoy sitting in my car. This isn't a cry for help, or to say I would rather like someone to help me "shuffle off this mortal coil". But what I really enjoy doing is to 'think'.

My big take away from this experience was a little insight into how my mind works. In the tank, rather than having a mind brimming with competing ideas, I had just the opposite: no ideas. No thought at all came to me, though some interior consciousness was there monitoring the whole situation. But to think took a lot of effort and I had to figure out how to do it, as if I had been cast adrift on some deserted island. Finally I lowered a memory bucket in an effort to find something to think about. Nothing came of that. So I mentally clicked down a list of my relations and brought up one of them to consider. But that's all I got: an image of them which went no further. Nothing I dredged up had any life to it. Nothing further was generated. No further thought came of it. And pulling the information up was an effort.

Frankly, I've had a much better experience lying on my back on the bed while waiting to fall asleep with the bedroom fan blowing over me. Thoughts of the day come and go. An idea flares up. A great elaboration of this idea begins, and then is put aside by another entering notion. And I fall off to sleep.

I had always thought of the mind as a very generative thing, in a Jungian way, with all sorts of metaphors and symbols and narratives and stories struggling to reach the surface to become expressed as things and light – as if the world were a re-creation of our minds. But it appears the mind is more aptly described as a little silent, smoothly running machine which produces no thoughts at all – until it is fed. My mind is much like my dachshund. I feed him and poop comes out the other end. I don't feed him and no poop.

So perhaps this old adage of 'finding oneself' needs to be replaced by a newer adage of 'using oneself'.

I'd always thought the expression "it makes you think" quite presumptive – as if to say that I'd had no thoughts at all until someone's particular point of view was pressed on me. But now, if I look upon whatever is pressed upon me as food - I bend towards that point of view.

If we want to know what we think, or to become productive and successful at what we do, or to even find out *what* we do – isn't it best to feed ourselves experiences rather than to take it on faith that some answer to our questions will miraculously appear to us from within a sealed room? I mean, I just tried this – if only for an hour

CRITICISM IS ALWAYS OF FREEDOM

Recently I happened upon this North Korean video which a visitor to South Korea claimed was clandestinely slipped to her. http://superchief.tv/leaked-north-korean-documentary-exposes-western-propaganda-and-its-scary-how-true-it-is/ As you can read from the title, this is a "leaked North Korean documentary which exposes Western propaganda and it's scary how true it is".

Well, I've watched this one video (there's a package of them on the internet), and I wouldn't call it Western propaganda. I'd call it snippets from a Western lifestyle. And I wouldn't call it scary. But, aside from a rather twisted view of racial matters, I'd say a lot of the footage is accurate. The United States – at least in the media – often looks like this. They talk a bit about Paris Hilton. I've never met her. They criticize Madonna, (three cheers!). But I've never met her, either.

How can the North Koreans know us so well? It's not like they get out and about so much. I'd say it's most likely they are repeating what the left wing has to say about the United States on a day to day basis in our own media. The North Koreans find much to admire in the left's criticism of the United States. And the left wing, in return, finds the North Koreans' criticisms uncannily accurate. You have to smile. The left wing and North Korea share so many values. Why can't we all just get along?

Indeed.

It's been said by a parasitologist that if you somehow did away with the flesh and bones of most animals and only saw the parasites that inhabit them, the animal would still be readily identifiable. This probably could also be said about human beings and their sins. Given unlimited freedom, (and a spray bottle of a liquid which fluoresces upon contact with sin), a human being could probably be identified as much by the innumerable sins he/she commits as by their fingerprints or blood splatterings) Sin thrives in flesh like a virus. It's in the nature of being human to sin or, (if you're not a Believer), to 'act poorly'.

It would be unnatural in a free country not to see all the sins of humankind flourish and be displayed widely. When our worst natures are given free rein to flourish and to describe us, they do – to a point. The beauty of the United States is that a person can see themselves – and others – as they descend to become, or by determined self-criticism and effort, can discipline themselves to be, and collectively, through self-imposed laws, continually re-create the free nation we enjoy.

The left wing would criticize us and our freedoms until we are beyond something lifelike… until we have become *something that only criticism can create, like North Korea.* The left wing would take the term 'puritanical' to a new level… a North Korean level. And why not? They have so much in common. It's uncanny.

BLOG ENCOUNTERS

Time passes in a library, at home as we read, even on the internet. Though it might seem as if we've slipped into timelessness, the people we meet on the internet grow older, their lives change, they wander away, or lose interest, or can die and are lost to us like a closed book.

Recently I was brought up short by a death notice on a blog I have visited from time to time: *The Baggage Handler*. His blog was an account of his life as an informant for the DEA; how he'd become involved; how he'd been flipped, plus the back story of his life. Abandoning Miami and his family in an effort to free himself from the habits of his past, he apparently died at a fairly young age of pneumonia in Minnesota.

Some bloggers, I think, are swallowed up by the despair of their situation – such as those ensnared in their own chronic pain or mental illness – and disappear. Or others, perhaps, eventually despair for their subject. For example, I found *The Chronicle of Artistic Failure in America* compelling reading. His interviews of failed artists living alone in their dingy basement/studio/living quarters with their failed marriages, or in deteriorating lofts stuffed with years of artistic toil and inventions, dust devils and mounds of old dried tubes of paint. Older artists discarded by the Culture and left to suppurate in their own health problems, in debt and/or swirling down the drain of their ingrown mental fabrications: crotchety, suspicious, bewildered and/or embittered by a vanished audience. It was like reading *Of Human Bondage* over and over again – without an ending. Now the blog is abandoned and drifting the blogosphere like a ghost ship.

A science teacher living in Peking, who wrote lovely scientific and mathematical examinations of emerging notions – spawned a lot of the 'emerging notions' in my own writing. However, the Chinese government and the smog finally got too much to bear. (He remained indoors, kept his doors and windows closed, and still his thinking grew 'hazy'.) The last of that blog had him hop scotching to Germany to get his life back and some fresh air.

Bloggers pass by my blog, and when they leave a 'like' or a note, I visit them. It's reminiscent of hoboes, during the Depression, scratching an 'X' on the gatepost where a sandwich will be offered.

I regularly visit a fashion column, *I Love Green Inspiration*, by an Italian woman just to oogle beauty, the clothes, fantastic settings and women. It's a quick lick of a lollipop.

A Brazilian blogger, *The Talking Violin*, with a deep sonorous voice, regularly posts a minute sound bite along with an interesting photo of what's making the news in this former portion of the Portuguese Empire.

An expatriate living in Bangkok (*Thailand Footprint*), regularly follows the local culture and expat 'crime noir'. I'd read a little too much of that, I think, before our re-visit there with our adopted Thai son.

A constant of mine is *The Culture Monk*. The blogger, Kenneth Justice, is on a "One Hundred Coffee Shops" stop of America. He flies, drives, takes a train, or walks perhaps, to major cities around our country and blogs with jittery fingers. It's a morning's cup of philosophy, religion, and culture via chance encounters. He takes the American pulse with vague stabs at the Great Questions. But he keeps within the banks of the cultural mandates, like most of the people's blogs I visit; like everybody, it would seem, out there. So debate his findings a bit, being a natural contrarian.

Then, of course, we all have to visit our friend's blogs to see what they're up to. Scot Bastian's *"Do Ya Think?"* is devoted to *skepticism*. (Those damned people have to be so *sure* of everything. We argue all of the time. Recent update: we split the sheets.) And Dan Green's *"Dangblog"* is a very well written perusal of current Ballard /Seattle existence. But as he recently voted for a Socialist, (which I think is like voting for a Tapeworm – why would you *do* that?), here again we argue.

And now I've just thought of another blogger I follow who is currently dying of pancreatic cancer! He writes a very good blog about art called, Robert Genn's Twice Weekly Letter – and currently from bed, so that his daughter is partly carrying on the letter in his stead.

But we don't argue!

MORAL OF THE MINI-CAN

Regular Garbage Can   the 'Mini'-Can

You Do Not Control Bureaucrats Anymore Than You Can Control a Roach

When I purchased my first home in Rainier Valley for $15,000. money was scarce, and I didn't intend to spend any more than necessary. So when the City of Seattle offered homeowners a lower garbage fee for using a smaller can, I immediately tried to sign up for my 'Mini-can'.

Well, a quick way for large organizations to cut their operating costs is to replace the job of phone receptionist with voice mail options. This has been a boon to government workers as it solves two problems in one fell swoop. First, it demonstrates to the public that your government bureaucracy *is* trying to cut back on costs *and* that they are underfunded (ergo sum). Secondly, it greatly decreases the time government workers have to spend responding to either disgruntled or demanding citizens – another cost-saving feature. In fact, if the voicemail directions are vague and complex enough, and the waiting time to reach an actual human voice long enough – there is a good chance that the government worker will never have to speak with the citizen over the phone at all. And nothing shaves costs like not having to provide the service.

So I looked up the number of the City Sanitation Services and dialed it. For a couple successive days I waited on the line until I could no longer bear it.

But I wanted my Mini-can. Mayor Royer, our mayor at the time, had created a satellite collection of "mini City Halls". These were *created with the intention* of allowing the citizens more direct access to the city and its services. So I visited mine.

My mini-City Hall was only 4 blocks away and situated in the local neighborhood business district in the shop front abutting the restaurant where I had my coffee each morning before driving to work. The coffee shop was an inviting spot which also included a bakery. There was a single cash register right out in the open where people paid for their orders. The mini City Hall next door was not as inviting. The mini City Hall foyer had been walled off with a very secure door leading back to somewhere, so that only a small space remained for a person to sit or stand. It was painted government beige. A wood rack on the wall held flyers explaining various city services and how to qualify. Half of this small front area was also walled off by perhaps an inch thick Plexiglas window, held in a log frame, with a 4" hole through which, if you bent down, you could speak with the person inside in a supplicating manner. Somehow, it seems understood (by bureaucrats down through time), that the person seated inside will not ask you for what you want. You have to get their attention.

(I forgot to mention that on the walls were signs warning that the swearing or threatening of any city employee would be immediately responded to by the police.)

The person, whose attention I had to get, was a middle-aged bottled mostly-blonde, with the beginnings of a middle-aged spread in a red dress who was painting her nails. Nowadays the first words out of my mouth would probably be, "Excuse me. But are you a real person or just a cliché' slouched there?" Then, however, I was much more contrite when approaching official power, and just said, "Excuse me?" She didn't look up. She was leaned back and probably assessing a particularly difficult ridge of nail at that moment. I continued, "I need to get a smaller garbage can? They have me signed up for a large one, which isn't necessary and costs more. So I need to change this and get a Mini- can." She looked up.

Not out of duty, but I think because I had piqued her curiosity.

"You want your… Mini-can," she said.

.With a lot of effort, she put her stuff away and rearranged herself.

"What's your name and address," she said.

I told her.

She picked up the phone.

"That won't do any good," I offered helpfully. "I tried phoning the Sanitation Department, but couldn't reach the right section and when I did – if I did – I was put on hold until, well, forever…"

She nodded, but continued to use the phone.

"Yes," she replied, when the person on the other end answered. "I have a person here who wants his *Mini-can*." She nodded, and gave the essential information. "Thank you." She hung up and turned to me. "Your Mini-can should appear next week," she said.

"Uh? Oh good!" I said surprised. "How were you able to get through to the Sanitation Department so easily, when it seemed like I tried forever? Maybe I could have that number?"

"I didn't call the Sanitation Department," she said. "I called the Mayor's office. And no, you can't have that number."

DAD

(1917 – 2013)

There are a lot of things which come to mind when I think about dad. I remember way back to farm days. He taught me how to milk a cow. He let me ride on the seeder during planting. He gave me a little plot of land to farm which was a triangle-shaped area created by the bifurcation of one dirt tractor path into two. I planted cantaloupes. I didn't think there were enough cantaloupes in the world. I loved them. I can remember only reaping one or two quite small ones. But they tasted great.

Dad also taught me how to 'set a siphon'. As memory serves, he was reaching through an electric fence to do so while milking the cow. Inadvertently touching the fence with the metal siphon while demonstrating, the shocked cow bellowed loudly and sprang, leaving my dad tumbling. I also remember the huge tumbleweeds that used to roll across the sage land. Getting anywhere when the wind blew could be like a punt return. We built a huge kite out of newspapers and glue and thin strips of wood which dad created with his table saw. We needed a rope to hold the kite in the wind, and then it carried me off the ground.

Dad also let us use fence posts to make rafts with which we fought 'wars' in the waste water pond. And he let us build forts in the baled hay. This had followed the disaster of our digging a fort out in some scrub land, into which dad had inadvertently driven his tractor.

When we first arrived, I can remember dad building our farmhouse with hand tools and eating cherry pie from a lunch packed in the trunk of the Ford. I used to step out back of the house after we were first moved in and listen to the coyotes howl just before bed. To my small ears it seemed like there was a million of them. Dad explained that one coyote could sound like a dozen. So... maybe only a hundred thousand.

After we moved to Spokane, dad left with mom each day to where he worked in the downtown Federal Building. I visited once and saw his fellow workers. There were lots of metal filing cabinets, rolled drawings, and drawing tables where a lot of his work was performed. He used interesting plastic rulers and triangles. He always carried a pen or mechanical pencil in his pocket. Whenever I asked him for help with a homework problem, out would come his pencil. Then he would find a piece of paper to use, before he began to speak. I never asked him about Tolstoy or Hemingway or Shakespeare, but if I had, no doubt the pencil would have come into play.

Dad always wore leather dress shoes with very thin socks, even when he was doing carpentry or shoveling snow. It made me cold just to look at them. He also wore khakis, which I guessed he started wearing during the war and just continued. And, as I've said, he always had a shirt pocket with a pen in it. He always kept track of the gas he put into the car or truck, the price, and the mileage at the pump. I continued to do this diligently long after I left home, scribbling down each item as I gassed up, until one day I asked myself. 'Why am I doing this?' I didn't know. But it was hard to stop. (Finally I kicked the habit by using the pen and notebook to record phrases for poems.) Oddly, he always wore pajama bottoms but a jersey top. Where did all the tops go? I guess they stayed in the drawer, starchy new.

These memories start to go on and on. Dad was mostly a nice guy. I wouldn't say that dad was an especially empathetic person, but he was basically mild and so endured a lot of arrogance and foolishness. Dad had a fine smile and a pleasant demeanor. In a conversation dad would always encourage me to be optimistic. But I can't say this was because dad was an optimist himself. I think much of Dad's good humor and agreeableness stemmed from the fact that he didn't expect too much. It's been said that one of the reasons lots of people have trouble with marriage is that they try to get more out of it than there is in it. Dad didn't try to get more out of life than was there. This used to bother mother. She would complain that he never had a "great time", it just went "fairly well". He never "loved" a meal. He felt it was usually "pretty good" though. I can't remember him ever turning up his nose or criticizing anything mom cooked. He used to wake us mornings by shouting, "Daylight in the swamp!" He told me once that the way he got through flying all those missions in World War II was by figuring he was already dead. Some people are offended by dark humor. I love it. I probably get that from dad.

Dad used to say that he let mom handle all of the little decisions, and he just handled the big ones. After I had had some experience, I argued one day that usually after all the 'little' decisions had been made there weren't any big ones left! He acknowledged that that was often true with a laugh. But then, being dad, I doubt he had ever expected it to be otherwise.

Dad was a pretty good racquetball player. His forte was to place a shot right into the corner where it would roll out. He had great placement. He got me running all over, and I can't recall ever beating him. Now and then he would play this loud, hefty, gum snapping, arrogant fellow at the club who I just wanted to smack. That guy loved to really put himself into it and would rocket the ball around several walls. You could hear the impact way down the courts. Then

Dad would place a shot into the corners where the ball would roll out down the floor until it bumped a shoe.

Dad's very acute sense of humor never left him. Even when he couldn't remember his last bite of food, he could follow a sophisticated turn of thought – and it would bring him a smile. It seemed odd that dad's recall got so addled while his humor remained. I think it was because humor was dad thinking, it was his gears turning. Some people might say that dad would joke too much, or was temperamentally a bit contrary, but to my mind, mostly he was just thinking. And the best thinking often curls back on itself. Every idea intends to produce "that which is seen", to quote the French economic essayist Frederic Bastiat , but also produces "that which is unseen". Dad's thinking would curl around to anticipate "that which is unseen". A few might recognize his comment's wisdom. But, "what is unseen" when expressed is often likely to be taken as 'inappropriate', 'impertinent', 'contrary', or just 'off the point' to downright 'puzzling'. So dad tended to stress the humorous nature of the unanticipated – or he chose category 'B': "Keep your mouth shut." Dad was fairly silent on many matters and left Mom to hold forth. Mom had a pretty big grip on "what was seen."

Dad's favorite portion of the newspaper was the funnies. He would collect e mails full of funny stories and events. However, I can't remember him telling a joke. He did with his humor what he did with his racquetball placement. He worked the corners. Someone would fire a verbal shot that blistered past, and dad's funny would reduce it to something which rolled out and gently bumped their shoe. It's a peculiar form of power, but it's the kind dad was given.

I don't have to go very far to remember dad. All I have to do is to be me. We were very alike. And I don't think he was very pleased with his nature, and so he wasn't very pleased to see me reproduce it. But as he was apt to say, "That's the way it goes." And, "Don't make more of things than they are." And we got along fine once I learned that relations with dad were like a marriage: don't try to get more out of it than there is in it. "Don't make more of things than they are." It's good, hard advice. We'll miss him.

HOW TO GET AHEAD IN LIFE

Are You Passing Up a Promotion?

Where I work we sell copiers. It's a large place. We are a large business with a big sign on top – and almost no walk-in customers. In fact, people rarely call us up to inquire about a copier. Now and then, someone new with very small needs will inquire via the internet. But basically, no matter how prominent your dealership is or how big your sign, in order to sell a copier you have to go find a prospect and meet with them. Our equipment costs a lot and has proven to be quite popular. But it doesn't sell itself. This is the first rule of advancement in life: nothing sells itself. Somebody has to tell somebody else about it. You want something? You have to ask for it. *You have to ask* people to do something, if only, "look at my stuff." *Nothing sells itself.*

Success Secret #1: Get Your Name Out There

Then, whether selling myself or a copier, someone has to buy. And to get that person to buy, you have to go to them. They rarely come to you, which means *that to get ahead in life you're probably going to have to travel.* Bob Dylan didn't stay in Hibbing, Minnesota. Bob Dylan had to get to New York where they were buying what he was producing. If you have a unique product to offer, statistically it just makes sense that whoever needs it will be somewhere else than right across the street, especially in Hibbing. *You're going to have to travel.* Maybe you're lucky and your prospect is just downtown.

When I visited New York City some years ago, what surprised me was how small some of the famous spots were. Greenwich Village was truly 'village' sized. Little Italy was, indeed, 'little'. And yet these spots marked the ground zeroes from where numbers of artistic movements and cultural icons have originated. This (plus some reading I have done) causes me to state another truth which is, that the leading creative activity happens within a fairly small radius, within a very small clan. There are companies who employ large numbers of people, most of whom use our copiers. But it is a very small number of people who actually determine whether it is our copier they will purchase. *Decisions about your future are made by a very small clutch of people who live and work and pass their time within a very small radius.* And you have to find them and get in with them if you want to become a part of it all; if you want to get close enough to grab the gold ring.

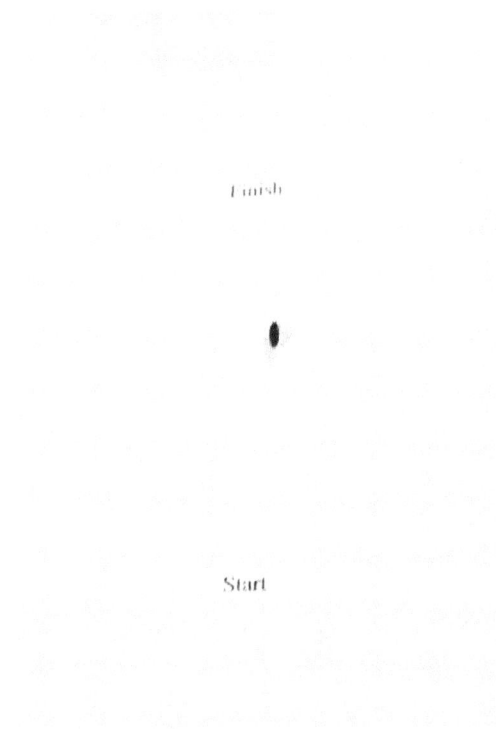

Success Secret #2: Have a Plan

As Woody Allen noted, "eighty percent of life is showing up". He meant that you had to have the work done and ready to go. But it also means that you are there where the work *is* done. So if you're a musician and you're in the recording studio, even if you're not employed as a musician, you're ready in case they need another horn, or if they are trying to think of a musician to call. As noted above, you're *within the radius.* Kris Kristofferson started emptying ashtrays and sweeping up at Columbia Studios in Nashville. When you 'show up' there is the possibility of something happening. You want to date that special girl? You first concern is to be nearby to give her the sense that you're already somebody within her community, who she might speak with, who she has 'seen around'. *Show up*. Be there! You're never going to get her if she is in New York and you're in Saint Paul.

All of this advice will work whether you wish to get ahead in a big way, or just in the smaller way of the day to day, especially this last trick: *Be of help*. You want something from someone, be it recognition, attention, respect or whatever – *being of help* is an excellent way to start. First, it's a nice thing to do. And second, it markets to the person's needs.

Wherever a person needs help is a place where that person is a prospect. And if you fill that need, there's a good chance they'll make a little purchase. And this works with anyone whether it be a wife or a child or a boss or even someone you don't know as yet. You want to gain your wife's attention? Do something she needs doing on a regular basis. You want to make sure your son obeys? Help him to do something he's interested in but doesn't know a lot about. They will come to rely on you. And people recognize and respect the persons who they need and depend upon. So *be of help*. Help to advance someone else and they may advance you.

(One caveat here: A little discrimination is in order. Be sure the person stands within a circle you would like to share. They might be in a circle you are trying to get out of…! *Screen* your prospects. Not screening their prospects is how 'nice guys finish last'. 'Caveat helpor': Let the helper beware.)

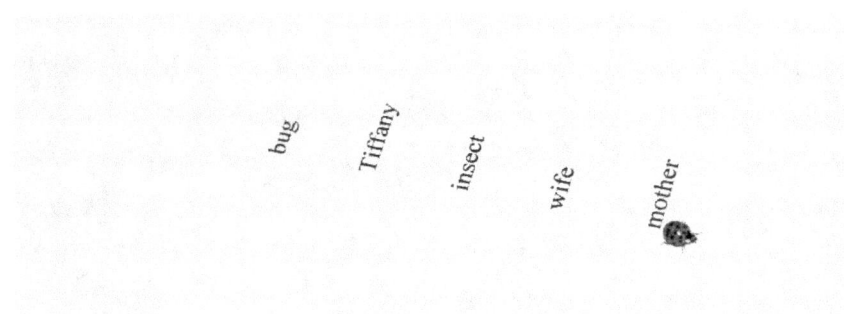

Success Tip #9: Who You Are Is An Ever Expanding Journey

Motivational Posters by Carl Nelson are available at:
http://www.imagekind.com/artists/carlnelson/MotivationalPosters
/fine-art-prints

SECRETS OF SUCCESS: PART TWO

When to Quit?

Portrait of the Artist as an Old Man

Too many artistic life choices and ahh-ha! moments have left their mark on this poor aesthete.

Self promotion will only take us so far. Sooner or later the Universe has to step in and promote us if we are to succeed. For example, I'm writing a serialized fiction story which I uploaded onto Authonomy, a serialized fiction webpage. I created my best cover. I wrote my best blurb. For a month it just sat there. It wasn't until another author noted, and recommended it, that I began acquiring readers.

I remember Merle Haggard announcing at one point that he was hoping to win the Entertainer of the Year Award at the Country Music Awards Festival for the coming year. Now I love Merle, but a notable entertainer he is not. His style is bluegrass stoicism. He's as flashy as a wooden Indian. I remember him saying, when he announced his ambition, that if he didn't toot his horn, nobody was going to toot it for him. That's pretty much how it turned out.

But Merle learned. And we can learn.

Most advice on how to become successful discusses what we should *do*. The problem is most of us *are* what we *are*, and so, we necessarily *do* what we *do*. Character is destiny. Human beings are not as plastic as those sitting across from us think we ought to be, or should be or *could* be. I know your mother told you that you could be anything you want to be. Well, if you still believe that, stop reading – or, more to the point, *why* are you reading this? Head back to Facebook and enjoy all those pictures of kittens. There is usually a fairly narrow range of activities which the normal person is good at performing, and an even narrower range of activities at which they are *very* good at performing – if, in fact, there are any. (A certain number of us aren't *very* good at much of anything. …here's a tissue.)

More useful advice would tell us *what* to quit. Because anyone with a little resolve can do that.

Success Secret #3: Know Youself

Let me expand. Before you become successful, you have to have been unsuccessful – or 'not yet successful'… And to stop being that, you first have to *quit*. An old Jewish household furnishings estimator in one of Arthur Miller's plays remarked, "The first step on the road to wisdom is to stop. Whatever you are doing, stop it." I can't think of better advice. When you remove something from your life, it creates a vacuum. And because 'nature abhors a vacuum' – this in turn employs the tremendous pressure of the Universe in a sort of jujitsu maneuver to re-fill this vacant space. The effort required is all on the front end, in emptying yourself of what is burdensome in creating that vacuum. After that the Universe acts as a big buffet pushing stuff upon you, until you select. Here again wisdom is required not to re-fill yourself with a past mistake. It's the same maxim as is choosing a mate: off with the old before on with the new.

So, how do we trim out the deadwood? A problem to becoming successful is deciding what to quit? Should you quit this, or should you quit that? Or, is it just a bit of this and that which you should quit? Understanding this will also help you to prevent acquiring

another mistake – it could even prevent you from wasting your life!
Something which hangs over all artists like the Sword of Damocles.

So, how do we trim out the deadwood?

One way is to ask ourselves what we enjoy doing? We are usually
fairly good at something we enjoy doing. So this first step is pretty
easy and quite enjoyable. Stop doing things you don't want to do!

The second way to prune your self is to look into a social *mirror*.
That is, try to see ourselves as others do - though asking them how
they see us is called 'prompting the witness' and gives skewed results.
It is best to just listen and observe. If someone says you have a great
ability to tell a story, then keep telling stories, and perhaps try to
contextualize other ways you have of communicating in a storytelling
manner.

Once a person discovers what they are good at, they simply need
to *do that with energy, and success is likeliest to follow.*

So. Here's my advice. *Just quit doing that!* Find where the deadwood
is in your personality and trim it out! Let the light in. *Let your green
parts flourish.*

Wife

Mother   CEO

ART WORLDS
BY HOWARD S. BECKER

As I matured, it occurred to me post-discussion that often groups of people had not really been talking about what ostensibly we were talking about. In book groups the conclusions puzzled me. It was as if while I was discussing the text, they were shopping at Nordstorms; holding up some piece of information or impression to see if it were successful.

Moreover, later I suspected that they didn't really *know* that they weren't talking about what they were talking about. (Definitely, I was puzzled what they *were* talking about.) I also suspected that they weren't having the feelings which they reportedly felt or *felt* that they had felt. Their expressions didn't ring true to me. And as I aged out, I also realized that many of my teachers hadn't lived the advice that they offered, and suspected also, that they hadn't realized that they weren't living the advice that they offered. So often, in fact, their advice was the direct opposite of what they were doing. Didn't they notice?

Have you ever crafted a very reasoned response for a discussion others are a part of, to find them pause and then carry on without a remark as if nothing had been said – as if you were a spirit which had drifted through the room, *shrieked* – and left, without a mention? As an artist have you watched artistic leaders make the most preposterous assertions without a blush to a fully accepting crowd? If you have ever considered the artistic community – or *any* community for that matter – and come away dumbfounded regarding something or other – this might be the book for you.

I am still incredulous that after all of the time I have spent *in* the art world, trying to *find* my way and to *understand* the art world, that it never occurred to me to *read* what a sociologist would have to say about the art world. That is, of course, they *would* study these things.

Well. I'm certainly late to the game, but I feel I've arrived. *Typing* and *Sales 101* are two courses I've always felt should be in any practical educational curriculum. Now I would have to add a third, and that is a study of the book *Art Worlds* by the sociologist Howard Becker.

Howard Becker's book is fundamentally about 'conventions'; about conventional thought, about conventional activity. *Art Worlds* discusses how humans utilize convention to organize and to 'regularize' production so that, in a professional arena, not everything need be discussed. This is the bread and butter of Becker's work.

In practice very little of any accepted convention is discussed. This is because the sources of conflict have already fought their nasty little internecine wars and spawned conventions which have been codified as standards long before you arrived. And people do their work within them like fish swim in water. Dissenters have long ago been herded off (and continue to be sent away) and kept somewhere 'beyond the pale', rather like Indians on reservations.

These conventions determine the flowcharts of nearly all social organizations. But they are very apparent in the arts where it is quite necessary that something nebulous be defined so that it might be crafted and produced and then be 'authenticated' (which is in the art world a way of being 'realized') in order to be understood by and sold to its consumers. "Art Worlds" examines just this. But as Becker notes, "the world of art mirrors society at large". What would look to be a good book for any aspiring art worker to study actually is a good book for any aspiring *human* to study. That is, if you would like to get on in life.

This is all about getting on in life. Becker makes no aesthetic judgments.

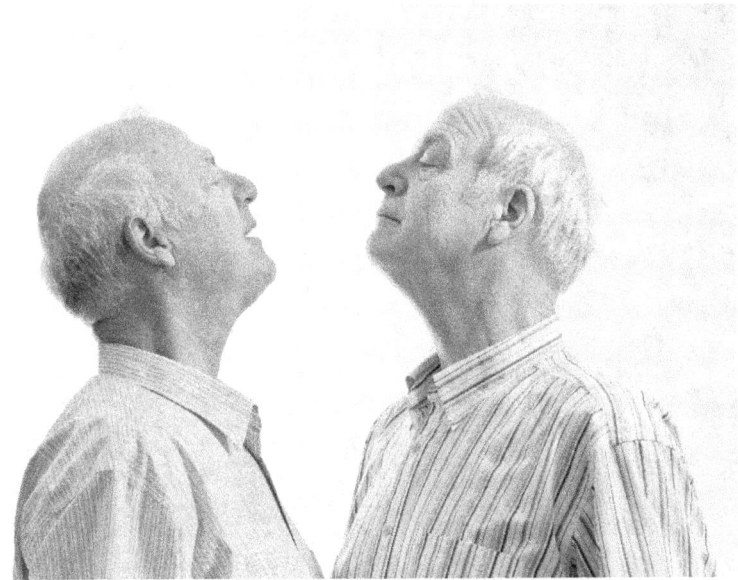

It's important to uphold standards.

When an arts organization tells you that they "must uphold standards", they really can't emphasize this enough. The life of the organization, their jobs, their professional status and their livelihoods all depend upon meeting the specifications of the art product they produce. To not do so would make the like blind Sampsons pulling down the pillars of the temple.

Becker doesn't theorize; he observes. "…sociology does not discover what no one ever knew before… Rather, good social science produces a deeper understanding of things that many people are already pretty much aware of." Becker, as sociologist, explains the functioning of an Art World in a way that those who understand only a part of it can't.

Art is Social

Becker begins his book by noting that "art is social". That whereas we commonly think in our culture of the artist as being the creator of the work – Becker goes to great effort to describe the community of 'personnel' who, taken together, produce the 'art' product. Further, he shows how the art cannot attain any stature without this community of 'personnel'. *Nor, can it even claim to be 'Art'.* As Becker observed, "Most history deals with winners. The history of art deals with innovators and innovations that *won organizational victories...* (my italics). Only changes that succeed in capturing existing cooperative networks or developing new ones survive... Art worlds routinely create and use reputations." Art worlds regularly criticize and defend themselves, authorize membership and reject aspirants. And they all define themselves, their places and their actions through an establishment of 'conventions'.

My first quarter playwriting teacher might have agreed with Becker on at least the first point. The first question our instructor asked our class was, "what is a defining characteristic of theater?". The answer was that it is "social". Becker continues though to extend this observation much further past what my playwriting teacher might authorize. In fact, Becker's exploration uncovers so vast an area of social involvement of questionable (at least to me) nature as to make this writer wonder, 'What the hell am I, or was I, aspiring to be a part of?'

It's a personal belief of mine that any true appreciation of reality is an 'unmooring' experience. T.S. Elliot remarked, "Most people cannot stand too much reality." In truth, most of us fight the Alice in Wonderland, topsy-turvy quality of reality. We really cannot stand to be too much a part of this world. We'd rather manufacture something with more stability. "That is our story, and we're sticking to it," is rather the nature of how we go about it.

So a book like Becker's "Art Worlds" – which can leave this artist/reader feeling unmoored – to my mind, is quite a book indeed.

Photos by Carl Nelson

.

POPULARITY

"While popularity is a trait often ascribed to an individual, it is an inherently social phenomenon and thus can only be understood in the context of groups of people." – Wikipedia

How much popularity is a single person due? How much attention should one person presume to deserve, below which she/he can feel rightly aggrieved, and above which he/she should feel blessed?

Tough questions, whose answer comes in fits and drabs throughout one's life.

According to Wikipedia some of the personal traits which are correlated with popularity are attractiveness, competence, and a high level of aggression. Social status is seen as a gauge of popularity. And "<u>social influence</u> plays a large role in determining what is popular and what is not through an **information cascade**. Independent of personal information, the information cascade acts as a strong influence, causing individuals to imitate the actions of others, whether or not they are in agreement. When downloading music, people don't necessarily decide for themselves what exact song to buy. Instead, they look at the list of most downloaded songs and decide to get those same top songs."

The reality is -as in the quote above – that popularity is much more a function of what the crowd desires than what the person is. Walt Whitman probably said it best: ""To have great poets you must have great audiences, too." And books could, and have, been written about what inflames the crowd – with all sorts of caveats and contradictory information tossed in.

Truly, our desires are a lot like that girl with a make-up kit, and popularity is the beholder who fancies that girl's wiles! Without a lot of glandular-ridden men, a woman's charms go for naught. Beauty needs those construction workers on their lunch break in order to shine. In fact, *we might describe art as the thing which would cause a person*

to act… which would fashion that overwhelming desire from within
the crowd.

Put this way, the popularity we are due, is due to the popularity we
create in an audience we don't know. And as a personal counselor
once noted, "most people listen autobiographically". So in a way,
popularity is like a charmed circle, and one is either on the inside – or
on the outs. And *that* is the popularity you are due.

This information is sometimes best taken with a drink. (And often
is.)

So. Perhaps a better question to ask might be, "How much audience
does a person *need?*"

Well, here again, it can depend. Say you're an entertainer. A large
amount of *paying* audience is required, or you can't pay your bills.
Your career ends. Say you're a business person. You need a certain
amount of traffic in order to move your product, or you can't meet
your overhead. Your career ends. Say you're in a marriage where
you need a certain amount of attention, or your partner does, or the
marriage ends. So here it is. We probably all need just as much
attention as is required to survive in the social net in which we
swing. We *need* all of the attention we want. Which is why we want
it. And when we can stop needing attention, we're fulfilled, and can

probably feel that we have – at least the necessary minimum – of all of the attention that we are due. ..Whew!

But, how do we *get* all of the attention we want?

A Buddhist might say that the answer is simple. We decrease the amount of attention we want, until the amount we have is sufficient. That is, if nobody acknowledges you, treat this as a *blessing* and a chance to live as unrestricted and freely as you would. Enjoy "the sun in the morning and the moon at night". Focus on the joys of pet ownership. Buy a fish, or go large and swim with the dolphins.

On the other hand, a Christian might say that we are urged by the Lord to go out and proselytize of His blessings; that this is our number one reason for being. Or as Robert Jensen has put it, "Christians serve a chatty God". "...a God who creates by word, redeems by an incarnate Word, whose Spirit delivers long, complicated texts to a community whose assemblies are full of words," as Peter J. Leithart in "First Things" puts it. And so, a Christian must go out the door each morning and find a way to 'knock the scales' from people's eyes! This latter can be the tougher road taken, as the Lord's work is never done. And people can be especially hard to button-hole - let alone fit for their spiritual glasses.

What to do?

A lot of people take the middle road – and enjoy talking to ever so many people about the delights of life – as they walk their dog.

THE HIGH COST OF MEDICAL CARE

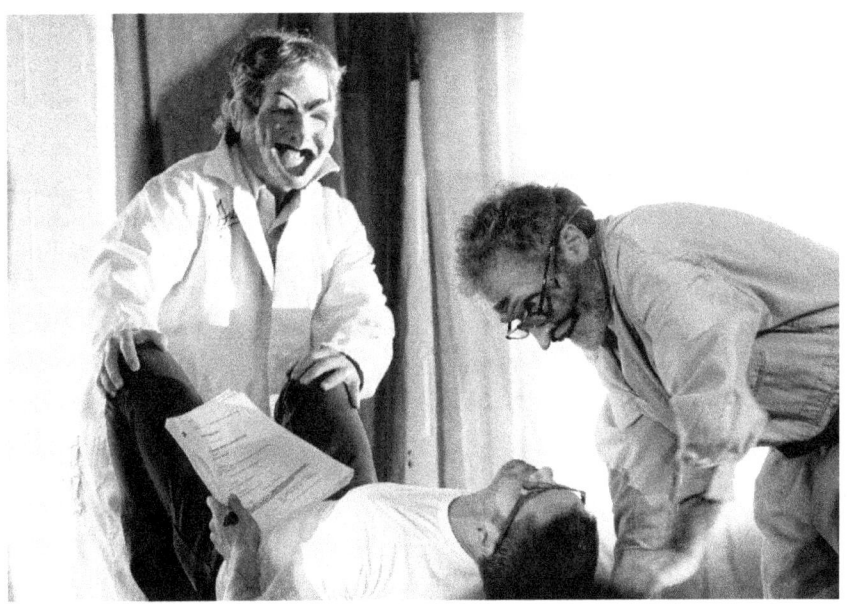

To increase the availability of medical care we must drive down costs. And *I can't see costs going down until medical consumers begin to shop.* Let me illustrate this with two recent examples.

Recently I had a long standing sebaceous cyst on my lower back, which had slowly enlarged and gotten infected, removed. The surgeon said the problem was right on the line between an office procedure and using a surgical suite. He would feel more comfortable doing it in the surgical suite, he said. I have insurance, so it didn't occur to me to inquire about the cost.

The procedure took 45 minutes of surgical time. Billing for the hospital surgical suite use was around $8,000. A bill for $2,000 from the surgeon arrived sometime later. Sometime later a bill for $1,000 arrived from the anesthesiologist. This is $11,000. I had no idea! After the insurance negotiated and paid their portion, I was still left with around $1600. out of pocket expense. This is still quite a bit to have a bump on my lower back removed.

I told my neighbor who said he was in his doctor's office and showed him a like bump. The doctor asked him if he'd like it removed? My neighbor said, "Yes." My neighbor said the doctor recruited two nurses and they removed it right there in the office. He paid $100.

In retrospect, if I had stopped to consider the expense of the procedure, I might have done three things. First, I might have had it removed earlier, prior to its growth and prior to its infection. Second, I might have opted to have it removed in the surgeon's clinic offices. And third, I might have shopped around for a better price. I told my son, for $11,000 we might both have flown back to Thailand for a week's vacation, had the lump removed and returned none the worse. He's currently watching me closely for another 'bump' to manifest.

My other example is my friend's experience which I will give you in his own words:

"I've had a blockage in my left ear since Feb. It was just normal wax buildup; I tried hydrogen peroxide and carbamide peroxide drops for weeks, but that only softened it.

I made an appointment for the ear blockage at the clinic where my primary physician works. They told me they'd clear out the ear canal with an elephant wash. I asked the nurse how much that would cost, because I'm uninsured. She said she had no idea and she would check. A day later I searched for "elephant ear wash" on the web and found the Elephant Ear Washer Bottle System by Doctor Easy <http://www.amazon.com/gp/product/B005M2B5P0/ref=oh_details_o00_s00_i01?ie=UTF8&psc=1> . I ordered one with two-day shipping and canceled my appointment.

The appointment would have cost $300 for the office visit + treatment.

THE PYRAMID OF RATIONAL THOUGHT AND HOW IT LEADS TO EXTINCTION

The Elephant Ear Wash kit cost $30.

It's nothing more than a spray bottle connected to a very narrow nozzle. I cleared the blockage in 5 minutes.

The fact that the nurse had no idea that their treatment cost 10 times as much as a perfectly safe home treatment—and the fact that I never asked or had to ask about the actual cost before—says a lot about the health care system."

And folks, there you have it.

Photo by Carl Nelson of a scene from the play, *Dark Farce*, by Freddie Brinster

"Are you going to stop my suffering?"

MERCY KILLING

My friend and I, whose homes are both plagued with pests, got to discussing what to do with a mouse, still alive, which was caught in a trap. I'd said that I took them outside and smacked them real hard in the head with a brick or a rock. I told him I imagined it would be like an Act of God, like one of us being hit by a meteor "…large as a house!" (with suitable arm flourish), I added. My friend shuddered a bit.

So I asked him what he had done with the mice he'd caught but not yet killed. He looked a bit troubled by the recollection. Apparently it was because it hadn't gone particularly well.

He said that first he'd tried gassing the thing in the barbeque, which hadn't worked. So then he decided to shoot it with a rifle. First he hung it on a board in his shed placing some thick lumber ends behind it. "But it's hard to hit," he added, since he'd had to stand some distance away. I asked him where he'd shot the mouse. "In the mid-section," he noted. "It's hard to hit!" He said again.

I imagined my friend trying to explain to a neighbor passing by what he was doing, and rocked with laughter.

"No one passes by out there," he replied.

So what would others do, I thought? So I searched Google to determine the broader public opinion on this matter. And here is some of what I found:

Dog hit by car with crushed hindquarters:

"Poor thing. I would call Animal control & tell them it's an emergency. Maybe they will send someone right out. Hard to tell with our government agencies."

"If you have a gun, kill it, one shot behind the ear, if not, run it over again, don't let it suffer."

"Maybe take it to a vet? I wouldn't though, it sounds like the dog is in a lot of pain. Maybe borrow a gun from a neighbor or get him to do it."

Some people leapt right into a moralizing posture:

Q. How do you put a mouse out of its misery quickly? My mouse is sick and needs help moving on to the next life.

A. "I think the one who needs help here may be you. It is not your decision to make as to whether or not it is time for your pet to die. You are not a vet. If your pet is sick, take it to the vet. If you can't afford to take it to the vet, take it to a shelter and don't get pets again until you can afford their care. It is animal cruelty to try and kill your pet. You could be doing it when there is a chance it could get better. You could do it improperly and cause more suffering for the animal. Leave the mouse alone and if it's time for it to die, it won't need any help from you."

Some people have gotten themselves into a hellofa mess:

Q. Can you get a mouse off of a glue trap without injuring or killing it?

A. ""You can dissolve the glue. Wearing gloves, add vegetable oil to dissolve the glue and, with a pencil, push the mouse off."

"put it in a shallow pool of water, not too deep so it doesn't drown, and see if the glue dissolves or loosens. maybe that could make it easier to get it off, and wear gloves."

"Yes, if you have access to a beard trimmer you can shave it out of the glue trap. Just make sure your rabies shot is up to date."

Some people expect a lot:

Q. What is the most humane way to put a small wild animal out of its misery? I mean for example injured mice and things. Sometimes my cats catch mice inside my house and I hate to watch them torture them to death.

Best Answer Chosen by Voters:

A."The problem is with your cat. Either you train your cat to kill the mice quickly   ,   or   just   get   rid   of   it. Why not try to teach your cat to be nicer to your cute little mice? Maybe if you got a vegetarian cat, it wouldn't try to eat the mice."

Some ring with certainty and authority:

Q: My mouse no longer has quality of life. How should my mouse be euthanized?

A:The only humane way to euthanize a mouse is by inhaled gas anesthesia overdose. This can only be done at a vet's. There is no humane way to euthanize a mouse at home. Asphyxiation by carbon dioxide, by drowning, or in a plastic bag; freezing, cervical dislocation, or feeding to another animal are all incredibly cruel and inhumane. The only humane way to euthanize a mouse is by inhaled gas anesthesia overdose."

Others sympathize and offer some simple tactics:

"I think wringing its neck would be best: However, it's hard to explain how to quickly and efficiently do this......Google how to wring a chickens neck and you will see what i mean. Or just give them a whack on the back of the head, its how many mousetraps work: Kudos for having the balls to do it: its a kindness."

"when i had pet mice and they were sick and about to die we would put them in the freezer. it is really sad, but we asked the people at the pet store and that's what they said to do."

"simplest and most ethical way is a bullet to the head, if you haven't got a gun then a hard quick strike with a blunt object also to the head."

And finally…

"Do it quickly with a shoe."

ZONING GOVERNMENT

Lately I've been reconsidering the Civil War. By allowing the South to secede, Lincoln might have not only established a precedent for forestalling conflict, but the energies of his Administration and the nation could have more productively spent structuring secession – while also laying down a workable precedent for the conditions of a re-union. Perhaps the Civil War could have been forestalled simply by issuing us all two passports and allowing its citizens to come and go as they pleased, voting with their feet.

After all, what are immigration and emigration but expatriot bits of secession and repatriation? And we allow it. In fact, more and more, trading one country for another seems to be the coming trend. A friend of a friend recently became a Danish citizen and says he 'loves' it. He's a big fan of their more socialized system. Relations I have are thinking of relocating to Canada or New Zealand. And there is still a large queue of people wanting to immigrate to the US. Why should we think that one form of government will suit all? And why shouldn't people be allowed to leave anywhere, whenever they please? And if we allow citizens to change governments, why shouldn't we allow regions to do the same? Mr. Lincoln, why didn't you tear up this war precedent?

The populations of the Red and Blue states currently seem separated most by whether they are urban or rural, large government or limited government inclined. Citizens nowadays seem to segregate politically around how much government they want. What if we could zone government so that people desiring a high level of government involvement could move to the high government zoned regions? And what if those who would like very low levels of government involvement could move to low government zoned regions? And we could define low/high government involvement levels by their total/taxed base percentage of the GDP – the thinking being that no organization ever grows larger than the amount of food it is fed.

We zone for industrial and retail business, high density condos/apartments, and residential. We love having more than one cable supplier. Wouldn't we like options to our current government supplier even more so? And wouldn't a healthy competition between government suppliers create better service? And if governments of the future were forced to complete for citizens (and tax revenue), wouldn't they naturally become more services oriented, less proscriptive and more enabling?

Certainly world corporations are choosing the governments they prefer, and shifting their incomes thereby. Highly skilled citizens are already choosing the countries they prefer. Why wait until we lose *our* most profitable companies and *our* most desired citizens? Why not start government zoning right here and now within our own borders?

Currently, if we would like to change our government or laws to address a grievance, we can vote (least work and least influence), write a letter (more work), buttonhole a congressperson (harder still), find an activist group which wants the same thing and join forces with them (this is like getting married – same amount of work and not easy to find the right fit), or get elected (requires the most work and commitment – and closely resembles a death wish).

Even after doing all of this a steep hill remains in getting your grievance resolved. The Koch brothers with all their money and influence have yet to be able to shape the government as they would prefer it. So what are *your* chances?

Currently our citizen appeal process is like having to change the entire management of Sears in order to get your dishwasher properly serviced. Wouldn't it be much easier if one were to just walk over to Rob's Appliance Repair and hire him to do the job? This is something *zoned government* might accomplish. If a citizen does not like the way their government is performing, they would be able to move where the government services more suit them. Moreover, a zone of government which is consistently losing citizenry might be much more willing to reconsider the services it offers and the taxes it demands. And all the citizenry would have to do to feel their grievance met is to move. Which is a hassle just enough to eliminate quibblers is my thinking.

Zoning would solve the problem many citizens and corporations are now moving to other countries to solve – without the problems of dealing with differing cultures and languages and laws and business practices. Why not legalize something more in line with pleasing everyone and quit insisting that one size fit all?

WHY YOU MAY NOT BE UNDERSTOOD

"...actors learn sooner than most of us that in the genre known as
real life, you have to present yourself, or play the part, if you want to
be understood."

– David Thompson, the New Republic

Have you ever had someone say, "I can't understand you." and
thought indignantly, 'Well, if I were paying as little attention to what I
am saying as you are – I would probably have trouble understanding
whatever it is I am saying, myself!'

There is much more to be understood than being clear. And there is
much more to being interesting than being insightful. And I can't
think of when I have been more struck by an observation, that by the
one above, made recently by a movie critic, quite in passing.

The ramifications of the quote above are boggling, really, if you are
anything like me, and have struggled with this difficulty your entire
life. What it seems to be saying, besides being like a trail marker
pointing in innumerable fascinating directions, is that in order for
people to understand you, you must have a personae or be in some
manner group-identifiable. That is, it's not that you might be difficult
to understand, in as much as you are difficult to *'locate'*. In other
words, there is much more to be understood than being clear. You
must be locatable in the brain I'd suppose. Like finding the right
word helps a person find his thought and from there connect it with
another. So, to be understood it would appear that you must
be *locate-able* in a meshwork of understandings the other person
possesses.

We all have experienced the all too common human urge to
pigeonhole, which I suppose would be the corollary to the above
observation. We often hesitate to fully speak our minds, utter certain
words, or even speak a small portion of our minds out of fear of

being 'pigeonholed'. That is, no matter the tack of our thinking, we fear it will be tossed into a some strange vessel of meaning our listener sails, enslaved and carried far away to perform some outlandish mental labor in some strange foreign land - perhaps even one hostile to us!

I imagine that the human mind must deal with rather complex notions in much the same manner my computer handles my digitalized photos. Each photo carries bit-packaged metadata, which explain just what the photo represents and where this photo is located in the database. Without the metadata, my computer cannot 'find' my photograph. And if my computer cannot locate my photograph, then it cannot *realize* my photograph. This must be something like how the human mind works. A person cannot *realize* your thought, until they can locate it.

So what happens to ideas that are neither group attachable, or come without personae? Do they drift about until the common wisdom catches up with them? I would guess this is very much the case. As an example I would suggest the case of Einstein's friend, the Mathematician Kurt Godel, who is considered "with Aristotle and Frege as one of the most significant logicians in human history." – Wikipedia

Godel has been described as "anti-charismatic". Though quite accomplished, he was a figure of little influence among the early circle of thinkers he frequented in old Vienna. Though he voiced much of what would later make him famous, little note was taken of him at the time – even among the very people vitally concerned and asking the very questions (over and over) he was softly voicing the answers to right there in the meetings they held.

DO IT, THEN STOP

Here is a *pleasure generator.*

I have found events of great pleasure in my day are either when I
begin something, or when I stop. For example, by the end of the day
I'm tired and sleepy and there is nothing better than brushing and
flossing and piling into bed, and then lying there in the dark to let my
mind wind down and exult in the soft mattress and the warm covers
with the cold and rain securely outside, and the calm rising up inside
while my dog licks my face and we talk. I remember that I have
money in the bank and food in the fridge, a wife and a son and a dog
and a cat, and a car that runs well. After a while, I push off the dog
and the cat hops up. And I rub him, feel the mats I need to brush
out, and we two talk a while in the dark. And then I push the cat off
and roll over and fall to sleep. A good half hour of pleasure. Cost:
very little.

Of course we all vary. And on a scale of "Do it" versus "Stop it", I
would guess I come down fairly heavily on the "Stop it" side.

Perhaps this is why I am so reluctant to commit myself to something
which is supposed to be fun and active, like a vacation. A vacation
can be hard to stop. They are hard enough to start. Jjust the
planning can take us well out of our way. And everybody knows that
vacations can easily go off the rails. Harvard Lampoon's "Summer
Vacation" is only one of a very many cautionary tales!

But nearly everything can be made pleasurable by employing my "Do
it, Stop it." *pleasure generator.* Probably even a Harvard Lampoon
Vacation. If you don't like something you're doing, then stop. You'll
immediately feel better. Or if you're bored, then do something.
You'll feel better eventually, and if you don't, then stop doing it! It
can't be simpler. And if you can't think of anything you'd like to do

– then do something you don't like to do… and *look forward* to stopping doing *that*. It'll feel great! You can't miss. You might even want to go for that little longer extension for a greater kick.

(Feel better?)

Really, this is a philosophy which always leaves the door open and plays well with other(s) philosophies and lifestyles. "Do it, Then Stop" is a team player.

A lot of people would call people like myself a dilettante, or possibly a flaneur (Fr. *trifler*), or for the more modern, a 'slacker'. To this I would give two replies. First *a lot of people* aren't very happy. And second, you can get a lot further if you stop to rest. (And maybe have a coffee.) Anybody should understand that.

In the morning when I wake, I lie there a while, thinking about getting up but not doing it. You see the trick is to stop it – and then all of a sudden I've done it; I've sat up without thinking of it. I sigh. I love to sigh. So maybe I sigh a couple more times – until I've had enough. Or maybe I'm enjoying feeling sorry for myself, so maybe I indulge myself in that for a few more minutes… casting myself as a great romantic figure, enslaved to some mindless duty, like earning a living.

Then I leave the radio on while I prepare. I sure am brighter than those knuckleheads who call in, and I enjoy the music. But if I don't, I can turn it off. And my whole day goes something like this. I make the commute interesting with coffee and a favorite radio show or music. And then I finish the coffee and the radio and the driving when I arrive at work, where it's good to get out of the car. It's good to stop and stretch my legs. Then I picture the work hurdles and jump them one by one. It feels good to land on the other side of each one and to get something done. Take a moment to look back. Or maybe it feels good to place something else on the backburner. Or maybe take something else off the backburner. Whatever. You get the idea. And then I'm a little thirsty, so I slake it. I look forward to lunch and then, when I'm done, I enjoy feeling satisfied. I pat my stomach, and then back to work to enjoy a short

conversation or two. And then I enjoy passing my co-workers in
good humored silence.

On the weekends, which is that big 'stop' at the end of the week,
there's nothing better than to start something. You get the idea?
You're always just playing one thing against the other. Say I mess
around in the soil and get my hands dirty if it's a nice day, or perhaps
I fix something. And then, when I've worked up enough of a sweat,
it feels great to stop and treat myself to a beer. Take a long shower
and clean up. Both of which make the wife happy...

(It *is* the weekend, after all...)

Or, if I can steal a few extra minutes, I stop downstairs and try to
capture a thought I've had swimming around in my head for a few
hours.

ADOPTION

"We're a couple of characters," the bearded elder said.

I was visiting my father over lunch the other day in an intermediate care facility. My father wasn't feeling so good and wasn't very communicative, so the bearded fellow pretty much had my ear.

"We're both adopted," he said, nodding towards the other guy. Which I found a bit extraordinary, as it was both of them, and then our son is adopted. Also, their adoption isn't usually the first thing a couple fellows in their eighties bring up.

"He's suffering from dementia." The bearded fellow nodded to the other fellow with the Albert Einstein hairdo, who smiled genially.

"He's a banker. But he can't remember where the money is. Can't remember where the bank is, actually."

The fellow nodded.

"Oh, well." We all laughed.

I told them my son was adopted.

The fellow said, "I came from a family which was dirt poor. There were eight or nine of us, all adopted, in a small town outside of Las Vegas. My father was Japanese and my mother was Irish. And my wife and I have eight daughters, all adopted."

He lived on a boat now. "I'm hiding from the world."

I said that I thought that sounded reasonable.

He nodded.

"My wife is a neurologist and each time she went, she'd bring back another baby. Until finally I said, 'Honey, you've got to stop going on these missions." Back then in the late 50s and early 60s, it was very easy to adopt. You basically just picked them up. "In Burma, at the brothels, they had the babies stacked in the corner. If someone wanted one, they just took it."

It took us three years and a lot of paperwork and education and travel to adopt our son. Things change, I guess.

"Back then, it was a lot easier to adopt children from Ethiopia. So a lot of babies got transported north and were adopted through Ethiopia. Everyone thinks they've adopted an Ethiopian. We thought we had. But then she grew, and grew and grew, until she was 7 feet tall! We had adopted a Zulu."

"She earned her way through the University of Washington playing basketball and then went on to medical school."

FOLLOWING OUR BLISS

"The reality is embarrassing. Being me just doesn't seem to get me anywhere."
- John, incarcerated sex offender

I had an acquaintance years ago who had just been fired from his job at a wine shop. I tried consoling him with those sorts of things you say: 'these things will happen', 'there are other jobs out there'. He replied: "But I've been fired from every job I've ever held!"

My older brother told me at the time, "There are a lot of people like this. It's very sad." ("They'll work for cheap!" Years later, I read a small construction company owner quoted.)

My favorite character in Sherman Alexie's new book of collected stories, "Blasphemy" is Thomas Builds-the- Fire. His mission in life is to tell stories. He's kind, gentle, wise, and tells pretty good stories. But no one in the tribe wants to/will listen. God seemingly has granted Thomas Builds-the- Fire the urge, but neglected the audience.

This strikes a little close.

Then the Bible tells us about Jonah, who really doesn't want to do what the Lord wants him to do. Ordered by God to go to the city of Nineveh to prophesy against it "for their great wickedness is come up before me," (Wikipedia) So he runs away to sea - only to be swallowed by a whale and spit back out to face God's admonition. It seems there is no escaping one's fate. (Hence, the word.)

Not knowing how to end this, I'll leave you with this anonymous note copied from an elderly man's Facebook comment: "It was great to see you in Great Falls, even if it was for a short time. I missed Saturday as Merilee slipped on the ice on our way to MPAB showcases and put her should out of joint. More than 10 hours in the ER followed."

The point? Life is oftentimes much more what happens to us, than what we intend.

Postscript: One reader found this essay a confusing "stream of consciousness". Though what I'd intended to point out by retailing these various anecdotes was that conducting your life by "following your bliss" is a little like driving with your eyes closed. Reality doesn't know (or care) anything about your 'bliss'. You very well might run into things if you drive with your eyes closed!

This idea of following one's bliss is borrowed from the Christian notion of allowing Christ to run your life, to my mind. Only Christ has been removed, and one's Self has been placed in the driver's seat.

So if one is watching out for you, a person should listen to themselves. (If you don't, who will?) But then, the wiser more mature person (in my view) considers others. A mature person realizes that life is a collaboration. You give a present; then you listen to see if that person really wanted it.

The Dog Psychiatrist is IN

A SAMUEL BECKETT KIND OF PLACE

"I can't go on. I must go on."

"The reality is embarrassing. Being me just doesn't seem to get me anywhere."
\- John, incarcerated sex offender

You needn't be a sex offender to feel like this at times. Tell a joke that doesn't fly. Make an observation which falls flat. Voice a comment which brings down a storm of contempt, and it's easy to feel like you'd best shuck your skin, or move away and start another life, or are walking around in a dystopia with a sign taped to your backside saying, "Revile me!"

But these are small quibbles next to looking into the mirror fifty or sixties years running and realizing that what you see was never *in* the running. You're *authentic* alright. And *what you see is just what you've got.* Where's the medal? Where are the rewards and approbation? Where is the approving God, Who has accomplished just what He intended, by producing *you*?

I relish the essay which digs a hole that just grows darker and darker until there is no light whatsoever and no foreseeable exit, right down to bedrock: a Samuel Beckett kind place where you "can't go on…" but you "*must* go on…" I find these sorts of essays relaxing. Because those who don't mind losers, who think losing is just emblematic of life's condition, and just one of those things which most often happens - are real friends. Especially if you feed them.

Okay. Return to the top of essay, and repeat until you've had enough. Then let's go toss that stick.

Photo of Distinguished Dog Psychiatrist by Carl Nelson

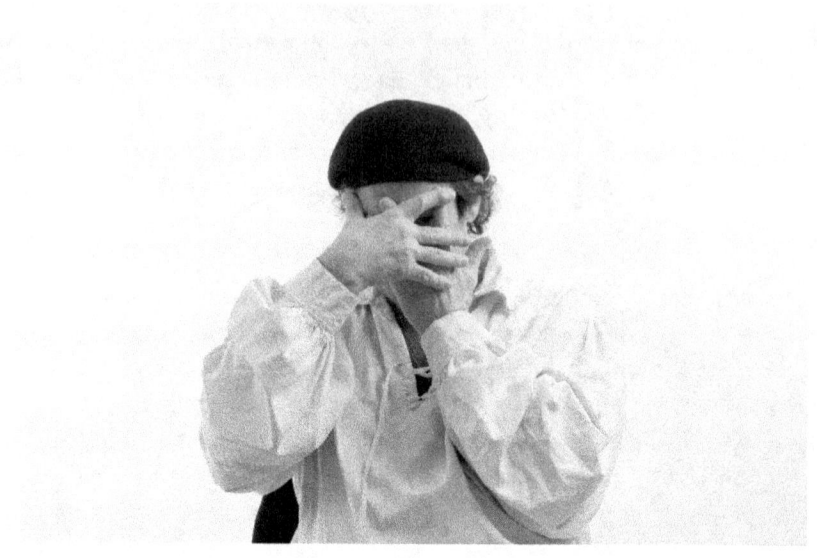

At a Live Reading, the Playwright is Often a Ball of Worries.

THE FUN OF LIVE THEATER

We had a reading of several small plays last night. A piece was read which a friend and I had collaborated on. Then a piece of each of ours was read. The evening went well. It's fun to write. It's fun to imagine. But the payoff of sitting in an audience who are clearly enjoying your theater work is hard to acquire any other way that by just putting it up there. The warmth and the fun of it are something to bathe in quietly for at least several days. And the memory can well be enjoyed for years.

Usually it's just a few select scenes which are so cherished; scenes where the acting and script seemed to speak and live so naturally that you treasure the memory as if it were a relation, or a wife. The play, as a whole entity, is usually cumbersomely remembered as part of the whole package of production materials: a concretion of crisis's, breakdowns, adjustments, grit and slog, insights, fear and loathing, people who fail you, people who save you, etc… rather like a life, out of which these special scenes surface like a State of Grace. These are what we work for.

There's nothing like having words breathing in front of you. Statistical hits on the website don't do it. Comments are fine. But after falling on your ass in front of people so many times, (which all playwrights do) a live success is something cherished. The whole room is happy. The actors are happy. The audience is happy. You're happy. It's the best sort of party.

Photo by Carl Nelson of model/playwright John Ruoff

MIRACLES ERASE THEMSELVES

If you are like me and listen to a song you love compulsively, until the glitter rubs off right down to the neurosis – then you might share my frustrations with familiarity.

But if you are also like me and relish relaxing in your same old living room over-stuffed chair and falling to sleep in your same old bed and being around the same people, then you also might share my experience that familiarity also creates a lovely.

(What you can't see is me taking a couple days to ponder this quandary.)

Wikipedia says that "A **miracle** is an event attributed to divine intervention".

This would indicate that it's not the event itself, no matter how remarkable (or *un*remarkable), which is its defining character. Rather, it is the presence of the divine. So, the miracle could come upon us quickly or grow upon us slowly...

But why do miracles disappear? Even miracles which reveal
themselves to us slowly (like the comforts of home and hearth) can
become a loathsome burden if we were to remain frozen in them past
their prime. For example, even I don't want to lie in the sack forever
and snooze or to sit in my chair *all* day. What causes this dissipation
of the miracle?

Most philosophers define a miracle as an 'unnatural event';
something which 'interrupts the Law of Nature'. However, for my
money, Baruch Spinoza's explanation gives us the more workable
insight. Wikipedia says, "In his Theologico-Political
Treatise Spinoza claims that miracles are merely law-like events
whose causes we are ignorant of. We should not treat them as having
no cause or of having a cause immediately available. Rather the
miracle is for combating the ignorance it entails." So, it doesn't take
me long to realize the beauty of a song I love. But I must sit in my
chair a little longer to realize the pleasures of the home and hearth.

This may sound like a modern day scientific/rationalist explanation;
that a miracle is simply something we don't understand yet. But I
would interpret Spinoza's explanation to say that we are ignorant of
God's presence in our day to day for which the miracle is a re-
education. That *God is merely a law-like event whose cause we are ignorant
of.*

Unfortunately, as humans, our memory of the divine is really short
term. You need only read the Old Testament for a continual
reminder of this affliction. We seem to have to re-live each miracle
as if born-again a thousand times. It seems it is very difficult for our
short term memory of the divine to stick. It's a wonder God hasn't
tossed up his hands with vexation and announced "these people just
can't learn!' Actually, I think He does this in the Old Testament – or
mutters words to this effect.

(Moses was recorded to have said by the tribal historian, "I grew just
to quail, when He would begin to *mutter.*")

Apparently God won't be captured, packaged or sold. We worship
an evanescent entity. It seems in this World, we must all get out of

bed, take out the ear buds and get to work if we want the New Jerusalem.

Photo by Carl Nelson

Between purges, show trials, gulags, and mass starvation, these guys
are just…

BAD FOR ATTENDANCE

If you're part of the ongoing discussion about why staged theater
attendance is dropping nationwide, you're probably not interested in
my opinion, but I'll give it anyway. Apart from technologic advances
- it's those damned pinkos.

Live theater has been rocked by technology since the advent of the
movies many, many years ago, and more recently by the home movie
market. But I think there are real parallels between the problems of
the American Stage and those of current leading newspapers' in
maintaining their readership in light of the overwhelming growth of
online media. In a recent piece by Keith Windschuttle in The New
Criterion, he notes that since a leftist cabal has striven to impose its
values on a couple large east coast dailies, (the New York Times and
The Boston Globe), their loss of readership as reflected in stock
values has gone from $54. in 2002 for the NY Times to $7.80 in July
of this year. And The Boston Globe has undergone a 90 percent fall
in value over the past twenty years. Meanwhile The Wall Street
Journal's circulation has increased 5 percent between 2007 and 2012.
He believes the lefties have accomplished this loss of readership at
the Times and at the Globe in two ways. By insulting the intelligence
of their conservative readers these newspapers have driven away half
of their readership, and by boring their core readership with the
ensuing substandard fare, they have also been losing their left wing
base. His favorite example is a story in 2005 about a seal hunt in
Nova Scotia written by the former NY Times journalist Barbara
Stewart. Here is a portion of what she wrote: "Hunters on about

300 boats converged on ice floes, shooting harp seal cubs by the hundreds, as the water and ice turned red."

"The truth is," Winschuttle reports, "she wasn't' even there and did not know that the hunt had been put off for a day due to bad weather. She knew so well what was required in a story of this kind that she could write it before the hunt had even begun."

That last sentence would ring true if written about the state of our contemporary stage. Most attendees of the larger theaters around this town know pretty well what is going to happen before they even go. To wit, some current shibboleth of the left will be polished to a bright sheen either by the play, or by the theater's take on the play. Conservatives will have stayed home because they realize they would be wasting their time. And *the left will be applaud both the play and themselves.*

Here's an example of what tickles the cockles of a local theater Brahmin. The Theater Director of Cornish recently spoke to the Northwest Chapter of the Dramatists Guild this past Sunday, where he waxed approvingly regarding a past production of the Intiman Theater which was about the practice of women's' genital mutilation in Africa. He exulted that they had full attendance and that there were even women in the lobby with petitions to help support prevention of this practice. He's talking about a big day at the theater - prior to re-organization following bankruptcy.

Now, in terms of full disclosure, I have never supported women's genital mutilation, nor have I participated in any. And it doesn't sound like a prudent 'best-practice' to me. And I understand that this issue probably really pisses off some women and probably fairly so. But... is there a real problem with this in the Northwest? Would I want to attend this play with my wife or family? How about with my mom and dad? Would I like to watch this play by myself? How many people enjoy discussing genital mutilation or watching descriptions of it? Would a cruel sadistic person enjoy this play? (Maybe!) Was this play really such a success, or was it just a success to the 'True Believers'? Or was it a glorious chance for the left to 'out' themselves – and cement their takeover? And did many in that

audience really care about genital mutilation? Or is the play mostly
an excuse to march out the 'usual suspects' and to tar and feather
them before running them out of town for the umpteenth time?

The Cornish don went on to say that he probably shouldn't talk
about politics, but since all of us in that room probably agreed… (I
voiced the lone "No." And the conversation continued, just like a
car does after running over a possum, or one of those Lone Star
pickups does after running over an armadillo when passing through
those vast stretches in the Red States.) The powers of this country,
he said, seem to be wanting to separate us into the ignorant and the
educated…. blah, blah, blah.

He went on to say that Theater attendance isn't ALL down. At the
5th Avenue and Issaquah's Village Theatre (musical houses)
attendance has actually grown. He thought this might be because of
their having the 'beat', the ineffable draw of music.

I think it's because at these 'musical' houses the public can still bring
their families. And when with their families, nearly everyone
becomes a conservative. And the 5th Avenue and the Village Theatre
know enough to respect this.

But, as far as I can tell, our Cornish don still remains among the
piously ignorant.

America's Finest News Source

MY CHRISTMAS PRESENT TO YOU

If you are one of those people haunted by the impulse to make the 'wrong' or 'inappropriate' remark, then the Onion could be your ticket. Or if you are a person who just loves to see the darker side of an issue represented, or at least hinted at – then the Onion might be for you. Or, if you're the sort of nasty person who just revels in satire, here again, the Onion might be your thing. Or if you are looking for writers who speak the obvious reality (even if it's not to power) in this politically correct day and age, without being tagged with a pink letter and marched off to that special place beyond the pale to be gassed later (okay, a BIT of hyperbole) – then the Onion might be for you.

A (lefty) friend recently remarked, "You are a puzzle. How can you love the Onion so, when they are so left wing?"

Well there are a couple reasons. Satire and sarcasm have perfected a style for promulgating the truth, which cannot be violated, even by the preferences of the writer themselves. If a satirical piece doesn't ring true; it doesn't ring funny. Match this to the Onion's, very often, impeccable writing skills and you get work of masterful observation:http://www.theonion.com/articles/guys-with-boring-jobs-really-hitting-it-off-a-few,30724/

Also, watch how the Onion can do an end run around the political gristmill, and let a little air out of the leading stories otherwise too hot to touch: http://www.theonion.com/video/in-wake-of-tragedy-americans-demand-reform-of-ever,30762/

Plus, it's just damned humerous about the personal day to day:http://www.theonion.com/articles/pan-left-to-soak-now-predates-all-current-roommate,30474/

So pour yourself a rum and coke and take a break from the Christmas doings with the Onion. It's a vegetable; so it's good for you.

You may drink water.

FASTING

Save Twenty Dollars or More! a Day by Fasting

Fasting is inexpensive. In fact, I figure it's saving me around $20/day. And it's a savings you can pocket right now! You don't need a personal trainer or a gym membership. And it's relatively safe, totally organic and additive free. Lots of people fast and have fasted throughout history. It's a well documented practice. Plus, it's a gauge of how much food we really need. (Not much!)

Fasting is easier than dieting. You need say "No" only once. You needn't wring your hands with each potato chip left in the bag. And fasting people lose weight without exertion. Fasting *frees up* a lot of time because you can fast anywhere, anytime, and during any activity. You can even fast during exercise. Fasting is the great multitasker.

Further, scientists speculate that fasting could possibly extend people's lives by 65 percent. So fasting is a powerful, organic, time saving, money-saving, fully committed, life enhancing, health tool! …available to all.

The toughest thing about fasting is ironically that it is 'slow'. Though 'fast'er than dieting. You can't do fasting 'crunches' for 20 minutes, four times a day, and feel great. It's all about time. And living with *loooong* stretches of time ultimately forces you to examine what you are doing with your life when not eating. Cultures are built and organized around eating and so are our lives! When you stop eating, you are tossed out of much of what (literally) makes us. So fasting *is* good spiritual exercise. When you fast, you realize how much of your life's enjoyment is spiritual – and how much is earthly. Mystics, hermits, and all the contemplative religions seem to value the emaciated figure who appears as if painted by El Greco. Sitting here fasting, I realize on what a drab, slender, tentative, and theoretical head of a pin my spirituality actually is perched. The mentality of fasting is like all of a sudden finding oneself in a world that is an empty room. Where is all the *fun stuff*? (Like donuts!)

Fasting is *not* making me a saint. On the contrary, I can get a little grumpy. But when you fast for several days, several remarkable things do occur. The first is that hunger does not grow ferocious. Instead it ebbs; it glides into the background of your activities, always there, but tamed somehow; domesticated. Everything eats! Even a paramecium eats. So that when you decide not to eat, it's as if you are standing tall and speaking back to Nature. Fasting really takes you out of this world.

And fasting also seems to make a person more contemplative. My body also feels lighter and complains less. Moving is easier. My thinking is calmer. If I were to judge from the way my body feels when fasting, I would almost conclude that food is bad for me!

It is hard to imagine that something we absolutely need could be bad for us. And also it's not hard to imagine, especially while fasting, that a cow or a plant is living in a *totally* ecstatic state. A plant is continually eating nutrients and growing! Perhaps we have no idea how happy plants are? Perhaps that's why they've not further developed any urge to move? Add another circle to Dante's hell! Perhaps motion is another indicator of a spiritual misstep.

These are just some of the thoughts I'm having 2.5 days into my fast. Plus, 'I 'm a rock; I'm a stone.'

Photo of model by Carl Nelson

Hey kids! Did you know...

THE HYPERACTIVE TEXTBOOK

Editor's Note: grumble, grumble....

If you have kids, chances are you end up helping them with their homework. When I was a student the texts had paragraphs and chapters explaining the material to be learned followed by questions to test whether we had indeed understood the lesson. Nowadays, just locating the explanatory narrative can be challenging. The page is a jumble of fonts printed in a variety of bold or normal or italic type and sizes. There are illustrations and photos and diagrams and insets and outsets and a matrix of colored explanatory boxes rife with additions and digressions and further explanations, and even little cartoony, happy learning helpers to point out important things you might not want to miss. All in all it's a thriving, teeming mass of intelligiblia (my term). Just locating the preceding and following chapters takes a bit of exploration. And the whole phantasmagoria makes me a little queasy. Whatever happened to simple schoolbook type and the narrative progression of reason... followed by a few well thought out questions?

Look at this!

If your students' problem solving skills are anything like my son's, it's a matter of glancing over the question and stabbing at an answer. And if the answer doesn't come in a lucky burst of insight, the next thing they do is to go looking for help. Actually, *demanding* help. (Looking for that little 'happy figure'.) Moreover, *help* to their way of thinking should provide the answer first *before* providing the explanation. Any *help*, such as my own, which has to mull the problem over – pause to think a moment – is obviously incompetent.

And this!
And this!
Cool!, huh?

As a parent we have to resist this tyranny of the ignorant. But it's hard when the text itself panders to it. To my thinking a good text implicitly practices the problem solving skills required by the questions. It is a calm thoughtful explanation, each of which parts are an equally important link in a narrative of constructed

understanding. It begins with what we know –
just as should the process of answering the questions – and
progresses in clear, thoughtful steps towards conclusions which
reveal much that we didn't know. It is an exercise in delayed
gratification much like a successful life.

But apparently our educators and their publishers all know better
now.

Cool! huh?

Photos by Carl Nelson of a professional model.

FOLLOW THE MONEY

(Our Adolescent Culture and How Discretionary Spending Determines It)

As I sat the breakfast counter this morning – over and above the lubbity-dub beatings of my inner contentment and love – it occurred to me that the majority of our discretionary spending is done by my cereal slurping son. My wife and I bring in a good income. But our expenditures are quite practical. House payments, car payments, every day repairs, utilities, foodstuffs and medical bills consume most of our income. That's my wife and I. Our son, on the other hand, has little income. But the income he has is spent almost entirely on 'new' products.

My son hasn't a lot of money to spend (though he does pretty well at leveraging mine). But what money he does spend is spent almost entirely on new culture: music, movies, snacks, designer drinks, concerts, trending clothes and sports. And while I spend much of my money buying time in order to produce the plays, writings, stories, poems, and pictures through which I hope to beautify our culture, …what I do isn't wagging much dog. My son, on the other hand, devotes almost all his money to *purchasing* what is new. And his money seems to be wagging quite a bit of dog!

The years have shown me that culture and politics tend to go wherever there is new money to be made, wallpapering our culture from stem to stern.. After realizing that my son does the cultural 'voting' for our family, I suffered a buffeting series of revelations.

You want to change the world? Don't go to school, study hard, work, and learn the difficult lessons of the life and all that – because all that stuff is in the public domain. Pushing this makes no money for anyone. You want to change the culture? You'll be much more effective if you simply go buy something from Wal-Mart. It's that 'Golden Rule': 'Those that have the gold, make the rules.' And my son's method is making the rules.

I've connected the dots and realize that the reason our culture strikes me as terribly adolescent is because it is mostly financed by adolescents; produced by the businesspeople who make their livings by catering to adolescents, and the cultural purveyors who pander to an adolescent's idea of the 'new'. As opposed to the Ten Commandments which God knows are in the public domain and reached market saturation lifetimes ago, (Don't even bring them up, you want to sell anything!), the 'new' has a shelf life.

Anyway, perhaps if I were a genius my work might charm our culture more to my liking, provoke a change or even get me arrested. For the time being however, the most culturally puissant thing I'm probably going to do today is to *shop*. Or just drive my son down to a Wal-Mart or one of the Big Box stores to *purchase* something. My simple action as an adolescent enabler will probably wield far more influence than I will ever have as an artist. Few will follow my art but most can spot and make change for a fifty real well.

Sometimes we're not the best person to present our personality.

OUTSOURCE YOUR PERSONALITY

Neil Simon, the playwright, has a face that is about as engaging as a cue ball. I find it unsettling to gaze at his likeness. His plays however do quite well. I've enjoyed his plays and my intent here is not to diss Mr. Simon. However anyone who has watched the Academy Awards has got to have noticed the charisma gap between the screenwriters and other behind-the-scene workers – and the actors who win prizes for performing their work. It's especially remarkable when you see them all packed together for a photo. You think, 'nebish', 'nebish', 'cool', 'cool!', 'nebish',…

I've wondered if playwriting isn't for people whose personal charm does not match their ambitions. Because playwrights are always shopping for just the right actor to carry their play. As a vehicle for public persuasion playwrights must find themselves faulty. Because they're always looking. They are always remarking, 'Oh, if I could only get _____ to play _____,'.

It's an unnerving process to hear the first reading of one's play. The actors rarely are what one hears in one's head. Inevitably you just have to learn to live with what another, hopefully talented, person brings. It's rather like having a stranger fill in a day of your life…. 'Jeeeeze!' you think, cringing while you watch a seriously bad driver navigate all those sensitively written relationships. Hang the head. Peer down between the knees. 'I guess this is what I'm going to look like to people. Maybe when he's done, I'll buy my wife some flowers,' you figure. However, after all is said and done, and the script swells with rehearsal, the script usually looks better with actors. After all, that's why you use them.

Recently, I found something better.

My son has only been in this country about a year and a half. But he is blessed with an unusual amount of charisma and stage presence. It's unavoidable that he is going to copy much of how I act and what I say. The other day I was watching him mimicking me unknowingly, and was struck, happily, by the result. 'When he says it, it really *WORKS*,' I thought gleefully. 'When *he* puts on my personality, it really sings.' It's like getting my wings, second class. What a happy thing to observe.

And also, kind of odd.

Photo by Carl Nelson

From "Saving Harry" with Nick Cameron and Daniel Woods.

GETTING 'STUPID' RIGHT

Editor's Note: I was thinking a little bit about plays…

The most important part of crafting a play is getting 'stupid' right. Plays can have great dialogue, ready wit, sparkling language, lots of drama, but if they don't get 'stupid' right there's a good chance it will not be a hit. 'Stupid' is that thing below all the language which makes everything move. Some playwrights are born getting 'stupid' right and some have to really work at it. 'Stupid' is what young people drink to become. 'Stupid' is what happens in extreme situations. 'Stupid' is what the young woman who has the handsome software engineer boyfriend over for dinner says, after she's heard about Moore's Law or Schroeder's cat at length.

"I think, tonight, we're going to have to get you a liiittttle stupid," she remarks coyly while refilling his wine.

Responding to stupid is something everyday audiences are good at, while cultural mandarins, sadly, are not so good. Cultural mandarins (and many critics) are like alcoholics. It's hard to get them drunk. It takes a lot. And when you do, it's often on stuff which will make you go blind.

Photo by Carl Nelson

DOES CHRISTIANITY HELP US TO THINK BETTER?

(It's what the evidence may say.)

It seemed to be a tradition of the great poets such as Blake and Yeats to fashion a personal cosmos of irrational actors and energies to describe the under furies of the real world; that is, the cosmological subtext. And poets various as Donne, Dickinson, Milton, Hopkins, and Elliot have used the testimony of religion to inspire and vivify their writing. And whereas we all expect of poets a little irrationality, it's little noted that the great Sir Isaac Newton was a practicing alchemist nearly all his life. Or that Kepler, Voltaire, Paine, Washington, Franklin, Tolstoy, Dostoyevsky, Edison, Gandhi and Duchamp held beliefs quite at odds with the modernist society they helped to create.

Einstein is famously quoted to have said, "God does not play dice with the Universe." All these personages had a fascination for the mystical which is scorned in our scientific and atheistically oriented age. But I wonder if such belief does not help us to realize on a grander scale and to orient our thinking towards what might be most successful?

Neurologists have found something contrary to what is nominally believed which is that rational thought gives us our best decisions. On the contrary, it's found that when the affective portion of our brains is severed from our rational thinking processes, the brain can reach no conclusions at all. The person's thinking is greatly impaired, seemingly rudderless. Apparently we need our emotions to orient and to direct us. So, it would seem to follow, that some experience navigating irrational feeling and belief would be of benefit to the mind in its entirety. So that rather than being just a useful tool to balance the checkbook, the mind can achieve its grander purpose which is genius.

A lot of modern thinkers are repelled by the chaos of irrational thought and by the infinitely ambiguous quality of myth, as if it were contemptible to contemplate with a process less than exact and more than ambiguous. But if we want our thinking to take us somewhere, doesn't it make more sense to anchor our 'vessel' to a current, no matter how deceptive and inexplicable, than a fixed buoy? How can we to find somewhere new, if we insist so upon knowing exactly where we are at each instant?

A religion's great benefit (aside from possibly being true) is allowing the believer to know where they are, even when their rational mind cannot identify any landmarks. Religion lowers the anxiety threshold. A strong faith helps us to endure when we find ourselves in strange terrain. A great religion is like a great river explorers follow to find their way through a landscape.

It's often said that all religions are the same and so should be equally respected. This is most often said, in my experience, by people who have very little respect for religion at all. In truth, there are great differences between various religions; and some are better than others. And how do we know which is which? It is the age-old problem of locating the false prophets. "By their fruits ye shall know them." What could be more practical – or even 'scientifically minded' for that matter – that to measure things by their results?

By this gage, Islam currently is looking like a few desiccated, blackened figs which smell of cordite. Buddhism is still hunkered around its rice bowl in many poorer areas of the world while pretending its mind is elsewhere. And Christianity is looking for all intents and purposes to have spawned a modern world.

Of course all of history is not yet written. But if you want to use your mind to its best advantage, to gain the best life possible, it currently looks like Christianity is the best river from which to chart the landscape. Why?

Don't know for sure. But it's what the evidence may say.

Photo by Carl Nelson

Addendum: After mulling the responses, I'm thinking... Hey, conflict is fun. But mostly, this tiny essay's urge is just to toss this thought (which had occurred to me) out there: that all of experience and happening is like rain falling on the landscape of our brains. And the channels these experiences exploit and the rivers of thought they create say something about how the brain has found best to handle this overwhelming onslaught of experiential data which rains down upon it every day and night since time immemorial. And the great religions might be thought of as the great rivers which move and channel this experience through our brains towards some productive end. And if these religions mark the best way to drain these watersheds of experience; perhaps they also give us an insight into how best to follow a current of thought to its most successful conclusion... any thought.

OUR MONOLITHIC LOCAL THEATER

As a playwright of 15 years experience, I've become conditioned to having my the hairs on the back of my brain stand up whenever I hear a theater worker gush about how much they respect playwrights. I imagine it's something in the realm of how an African-American reacts wherever someone remarks, "Oh, I just love Black people!" They suspect that somewhere in this person's experience there has been a great black *maid*... truly one of the *family*.

Because my experience in the Theater has been that most theaters like their playwrights either dead or out of town. Directors will declare it can't "be done" that way. Dramaturges will insist that ignoring their advice is tantamount to intentionally blemishing their career. And the Producers will say that if they do not get their way, although they love the play so much!! the production will be cancelled; the play will be dropped. If the playwright is not dead, or out of town – they may soon want to be.

 This is because most mid to high end theater nowadays is not creative. They are production entities. They are like the copyists of the old-time Louvre. Known, established hits of the recent season are imported, and the theaters' job is not to fuck them up. The critics report on how well they have done this. "Yes! In this production they magically recreate the flair of Titian's brushwork." It's educational.

Copyists

WELL, all that has changed! according to a recent article in the Seattle Times by theater critic Misha Berson: *"Move over, coffee: It's playwrights' day in the sun in Seattle"*. The larger theaters all say so! And, *apparently*, it's all come upon us quite suddenly.

Three months ago in a meeting of the Dramatists Guild at the ACT Theater, representatives from the Rep, ACT, Issaquah's Village Theatre, and the 5th Avenue, announced that they were now intent upon establishing playwriting entities within their theater's organizations in order to foster the creation, workshopping and *perhaps* production of New Plays.

I asked them a number of questions *then*. First, why all of a sudden? Local playwrights have been doing everything short of tossing bombs at their doors for the past 15 years of my experience in an effort to make just this sort of thing happen. Their non-committal answer was just a general shrug and a few general statements to the effect that, the time seems to be right, or it seems to be what is currently *in the air*.

Well, who can really say?

THE PYRAMID OF RATIONAL THOUGHT AND HOW IT LEADS TO EXTINCTION

(This writer suspects that it is the money. You want to understand any organization, you follow the money. And major theater in this town has seen patrons and income steadily decrease in numbers over the past many years. At the next Dramatists Guild meeting the Artistic Director of another major theater in the area said that she had had to let all of her assistants go. If this is true throughout the industry, then the next jobs to be lost are going to be those of the very people who were speaking to us. **This** *can be a motivator.*

But why, suddenly, are they so chummy with playwrights? WE haven't any money. Trust me.

I suspect it's either due to a major change in grant or funding priorities among the philanthropic entities, though your erstwhile reporter here has come up blank. Perhaps they are just getting desperate and are casting about wildly in their death throes like large animals. Or perhaps, when you take the money away, people become creative... or at least open themselves up to the idea.)

Well, part of the answer is that they are not really chumming up. They are *allowing* the playwrights into their theater. When asked the benefits of this, the lone playwright of the group who was part of this newly hatched program said, "Well, I get to talk to other playwrights." He thought for a while. "And I get to use the copy machine."

Let's see. "I get to use the copier machine."

(Hallelujah! I thought. The grant is large enough that we can talk to each other.)

They all made it very clear that they were not just opening the theater doors ala carte. They planned to contact select writers with invitations. These writers would then be allowed to work and talk with other writers somewhere on the theater grounds. And out of all of this, if the powers that be deemed the product of sufficient quality, some portion of this would at some point have scheduled readings – when they could be arranged, *if* the budget was there for them. And hopefully from this might come some productions. (Smiles all around.)

('I could scratch something out today, have it read down at the Odd Duck tonight, and in a show there, or in the TPS Theater by the end of the next month!' My ears were blowing smoke. 'And all without having budgeted a dime. A STREET person could do this.')

Odd Duck Theater
SEATTLE, WASHINGTON

And in case they had qualms about the dubious quality of such work coming out of a rundown place such as the Odd Duck? I would remind them that the two playwrights they so prized, and had produced upon their own stages, and had been just now passing congratulations back and forth about – had passed through just such a scenario at the Odd Duck, in years past, themselves.)

So I asked them, "Why not just save your selves a lot of time and effort and money and just cut to the chase? Go see the shows produced around here which have done well and give them a leg up?"

(I didn't add, "Because that's what you do - with shows from elsewhere - already!")

It was not just a question of quality, was their answer. It was also finding the show which was right for their theater.

"But in ten years you haven't yet found a show which was right for your theater?" I asked.

Believe us, we've looked, was their answer.

(This is the kind of bloviate which they had been tossing us for ten years.)

"But Joe Boling, an independent fellow who had tried to see how much theater he could attend within the Seattle area within a year, by attending every day… (They all nodded their heads and smiled. They all knew the guy.) …found he couldn't see all of the productions, within a year, there were so many! You couldn't find one success out of all of those *produced* scripts, over the past 10 years which was suitable?" I asked again.

??????

Believe us, we've looked, was their answer.

They didn't blink. They didn't break ranks. You've got to hand it to them, when it comes to political gamesmanship these folks know their way around. They appear when they are invited, and then they come bearing gifts – to mute any criticism which might rear its ugly

head. And it had muted me. What I should have continued on to
ask was this:

*("Let me phrase this question another way – since it seems you have to be hit on
the head with a big stick! If local theater producing new, local plays
has* **created audience** *with a series of hits – while your theaters have been
steadily* **losing audience**... *Wouldn't it be more logical to say that* **perbaps
your theatre is not 'right' for this town?")**

But they propped their sagging tits of an argument up this time with
a few anecdotes about how time consuming and taxing watching new
theater could be. Which led to the condolences passed amongst
themselves, (they were all on good relations), regarding sacrifices that
a (salaried) person makes for the theater...

So I figured that was enough questions from me for a while. Since
no other playwrights attending followed up on my queries, I just sat.

The other playwrights asked questions about how one became picked
by a theater; how one should best submit their work to the theater,
and on and on; just dogs, basically, who were sitting on their hind
legs asking politely what the protocol was to be for chasing the bone.
And one thing the panelists agreed upon was that there was no
equation to give! They were looking for quality, and then something
which tugged at their heart. But one thing we could do was to
research the theater we were sending our scripts to.

*(A little background here: The Dramatists Guild recently supported a study of
the state of live theater in this country, which caused somewhat of a sensation when
it came out around a year ago. Not only was it shocking how little even quite
'successful' playwrights made from their theatrical productions (barely a blue collar
income). What struck closest to many of us (especially me!) was the finding that
there were no scripts produced in major theaters around the country from
mailings. The playwrights in all cases that were produced had a personal
relationship with that theater.)*

For example, said the fellow from the largest theater. If I receive a
script and it has blah, blah, blahs name on it. I know that that person

93

hasn't researched our theater at all, because blah blah blah hasn't been the literary manager here in several years. So into the round file it goes...

"You're kidding me. That pre-schooler thinks MARK is still the Literary Manager?"

(The arrogance of these people just twists me in knots. At ten cents a sheet, the playwright may have spent $12.00 for the copy, another several dollars for the binder, maybe $3.00-$6.00 for the postage, and then double that amount for the return envelope and postage. This is not to mention the year (or years) and turmoil spent to write it.)

So I had to ask: "So, after you have produced a new play, how do you go about selling it to the other major theaters. Do you just make sure you get the names correct and mail it to them?"

Oh no, no. We try in every way we can to get them here to see it!!!

About this they all agreed.

And then it was pretty much over. I left without speaking. If I did start talking, I wasn't sure I'd be able to stop. And also, it was pretty clear that neither the panelists nor the other playwrights were much interested in what I might have to say, might be.

But to finish up, I think I'll just say what I have to say right here:

I agree with Jon Jory (founder of the Humana Festival) that the future of live theater is probably at the amateur, semi-professional level of production. What I see happening here are the deaths throes of a large, monolithic creation which is currently stumbling under its own weight, and fighting to retain what employment there is. Large theater as we know it is going down... It's getting re-sized, re-packaged. Who knows, maybe even chopped up for its parts...

(An administrator's arm... maybe a head?   Might I swing the axe?)

But theater as it's about to be will be coming to your block. And who knows? Maybe soon.

And more about that, later.

Photos by Carl Nelson of persons and actors whose sentiments may very well not be mine.

MONOLITHIC LOCAL THEATER CONTINUED...

LEVEL ORANGE

If you've ever had a job you can understand how water runs uphill. The boss says so, and the workers all nod and marvel.

This is a bit how I felt after reading in this past week's Puget Sound Business Journal: "The Seattle area has a long history of supporting new theatrical works, often with great success on Broadway and elsewhere. Now the drive that built that legacy is gaining momentum with new programs and investment in cultivating art at its earliest stages." (I shake my head and marvel.)

"It's part of a strategy that brings money back to local theaters that own the rights to the new works," continues Valerie Bauman, staff writer. "For example, 5th Avenue's "Hairspray" has generated more than $1 million in royalties since it was picked up on Broadway." (I *nod* my head this time, *with greater understanding…*)

I have to say that it's all part of a strategy that's beginning to take on a form, here in Seattle, as the local news continues to fluff it up.

In my first piece here in *The Editor's Perch* on "Our Monolithic Theater", I pointed out that regional theaters here and elsewhere have no record of ever producing a mailed play script – unless that playwright first had a relationship with the theater. It was also shown that our local theaters refused to pick up local shows which were clear hits, responding that they had never found one which was *right for their theater.*

Now, it's become plainer what makes a play '*right for their theater'.* It's pretty simple, really: **THEY** *own the rights.* (And they get the million dollars.)

In return, as was covered in our last piece, the playwright gets to talk to other playwrights, access to their copy machine, and also a reading… if monies can be found, and patience is acquired. All these things, I *repeat*, which could be accomplished (and probably *has* been accomplished) by the playwright him/herself within a few days around here – even if they were living out of a box on the street.

The New Works Program at the 5th Avenue Theater, however, is promising a little more: "The program also provides an opportunity for artists to get feedback and exposure at the earliest phase of creating a script, a song or a performance. *Along the way, they're paid for their work. (This is a pleasant sounding way of saying, along the way you are selling your rights to the work for peanuts, so that we get the royalty money and write the plays destiny.)*"

This is the Brave New World of our Regional Theater. And it gripes me.

I try to get my son to eat more naturally made bread, but he likes white bread. I point out to him that bread with all sorts of whole wheat and grains still has much of the natural nutrition you should seek in a meal. But he points out *to me* the laundry list of nutritional additions, almost as long as his forearm, listed on the side of the white bread plastic sack – while the list on the side of *my* bread sack is ever so small.

Institutions are like my son. They prefer white bread. It's soft; it goes down easy; it hits that golden mean and it's got all of its benefits listed right there on the side for all to see. It has 'proof' that's it's nutritional sound and will build your body in "12 different ways." All 'natural' bread has is that it's natural. Its list of ingredients is very short.

Not long ago I saw a matinee production of the "Pullman Porter Blues" by Cheryl L. West produced by the Seattle Rep. The set was good; the acting was good; the direction was good; and the writing was good. But the story was boiler plate liberal. The regional theaters have been refining this formula for as long as I have been alive. The play was **4 years** in development. And I imagine in 4 years a regional theater could really leach out all the natural nutrition a fresh script provides and replace it with politically pure proven supplements. You may have experienced the audience this sort of racial testimony play attracts: a lot of White people who nod and say, "aaahhh!", as they notice each of the ingredients the playwright has posted on the side of the package. And then there is a smattering of well-dressed somber Black people. And God knows what they are thinking.

Contrast this with the plays of another Black playwright, Tyler Perry, whose plays went from small church productions to major venues which attracted Black people by the droves. His plays weren't *right* for the regional theaters. Or more recently contrast this with the plays of Black playwright Thomas Bradshaw, whose "Job" now runs at the Flea Theater – a private theater run by the husband of the actress Sigourney Weaver – through November 3rd in New York City. His material "is best described as life with all the ghastly extremes – incest, rape, racially motivated murder – added back in and depicted in a deadpan style that has prompted both big laughs and angry walkouts," says the New York Times. I'm doubting this play had 4 years of development. It sounds like it was popped right out of the oven… or rather it grew beyond all bounds in the writing and overflowed the oven and onto the stage.

Being a writer, all I really want is to have my say, and I've had it. I can't say I've attracted either the audience or critical approval to fill a larger venue, even if one of our regional theaters were to approach me. I'll practice my craft elsewhere, thank you. As long as people love to perform there will be live theater. So look around, I may be there. All we need is "two boards and a trestle."

HOW TO CATCH AND KILL A FLY WITH YOUR BARE HAND

You needn't be fast. It's a question of creating the trap and then, timing! (But having a large hand may be a plus.)

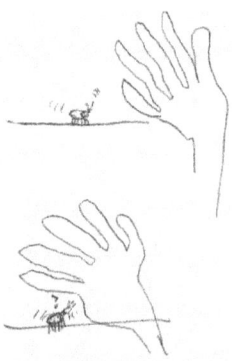

Figures 1 & 2

First approach the sitting fly with your dominant hand. (See figure 1.) Notice that the fingers are moderately spread, like the bars on a cell.

As your hand gets closer to the fly, the fly must decide what to do. (See figure 2.)

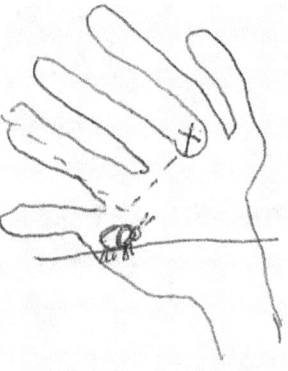

Figure 3

The fly will act when your hand is within a certain distance. (See figure 3.) If the distance to safety is made shorter by flying between your fingers, then this is the direction in which the fly will fly.

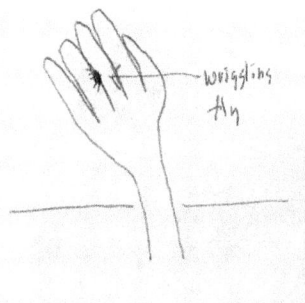

Figure 4

By trying to trap the fly repeatedly, you will discern at what distance the fly will make his move. You need simply to begin closing your fingers together slightly before this distance, and then tightly as you continue… and the fly is yours! (See figure 4.)

Illustrations by Carl Nelson

Editor and His Dog Camping

MOSS

Editor's note: Have your wife and neighbors ever asked you to go out and kill something you love?

I'm a big fan of moss. Moss is cool, soft, green and makes for a lovely ground cover while discouraging weeds. Moss dates from pre-history and has retained its nature for millions of years being just about as old as the little arthropods which crawl across it. Moss arrived most probably just after the seventh day, perhaps as an afterthought, as you will find moss on graves, in nooks and crannies, and on the rear-end of things.

Moss is the sort of plant which will suffer fools. Moss is what is left after we've done all the 'important' things we are going to do. We've made that name for ourselves. We married the leggy blonde and spawned that far above average family. We have more money. Our politics make theirs look like Lincoln logs. Our kids have done better than their kids. Plus! ours can kick their ass, and we won WWII... did we mention? After all the political infighting, moss is left to coat everything in a lovely, romantic emerald green, kind of like all those dead Irish partisans of memory.

Moss is the sort of plant which will get right down in the dirt and strive for the personal contact. Moss is not, 'Look at me, I'm lording it over you. 'Cause you're short and pale and lazy, besides.' Not that kind of vegetation shaming for moss. Nope. Moss does not preen, but has an eye for timeless value. Moss-type people find other's preening and affectations as a substrate to build upon. And in the end they shall turn it into something nice, and soft and green...

romantic, even. There's an endless task for you - requiring an abiding patience.

Photos by Carl Nelson

WALKING THE STREETS

I complained to a friend of mine about a brief encounter with a
vagrant on a downtown street who had pestered me into
conversation. "It's so corrosive to the social fabric, so deleterious to
the social compact people require in order to care for one another," I
complained. "This guy comes up to me and starts his friendly
conversation like he wants to know me. And as soon as he figures
I'm not giving him any *money*, he leaves. Or if I do give him money,
he only chats further as long as he figures he might get more, and
then he leaves. He doesn't care a fig about me or want to know me
at all!"

My friend laughed. "Of course he wants your money. What do you
expect? He's living on the street! You have the money, and they
don't." He spoke with the assurance of a professional social worker.
"How do you think they're going to act?" He looked at me as if I
were naive.

Well, nevertheless, I think it makes a great deal of difference how people *do* act. If I were to tell my friend that in my experience, the *real* reason people end up on the street is not because they run out of money, but because they run out of friends – he would no doubt laugh with scorn and say, 'The *real* reason they are out on the street is because they are flat broke!'

My friend believes what is needed is a total economic transformation of our current system and much more government involvement. And this will come with more education of the electorate.

Not that my friend is going to help them. In fact, he just shook his head when I gave one of these scam artists money!

But some of these street fellows: they show a bit of sales skills; we have a little fun parrying, they're good story tellers or actors; maybe they are just shy or I admire their stoicism; or they are just pathetically so over the top! As an aspiring theater person, I just feel I just have to toss some money in the hat for that. I'm not supporting a drunk; I'm supporting the Arts.

Photos by Carl Nelson

THE REPUBLICAN THEATER FESTIVAL

http://nycp.blogspot.com/2012/07/republican-theater-festival.html

My friend Scot sent me this link, even though it made him "gag" bless his soul (that he denies he has).

Anyway, any pro-Republican stance is such an odd event in the live theater community that it has gotten some press: http://blogs.phillymag.com/the_philly_post/2012/07/26/republican-theater-festival/

The last theater I've heard of which offered a platform for Republican ideas was the year the Humana New Theater Festival produced by the Actors Theatre of Louisville offered William Buckley a play spot in the line-up (1988-89). This was a nationally recognized event which brought enormous media attention to the Louisville Theatre. Which was just what the festival founder and the idea's originator, Jon Jory, had had in mind. When Jory spoke to the Seattle contingent of The Dramatists Guild in 2011 he said that his thinking was that if theater is drama involving everybody, why not bring the one contingent which was not currently represented on the stage to the Festival? He got what he wanted, but he added that it was "5 years before some people at the Humana would speak with me".

Anyway, we haven't travelled *any* distance since then! So perhaps progressives *are* as bright as they believe they are. Because political theater nowadays is still what it was in those days: agitprop, show trials, or puff pieces for the latest liberal topic d'jour, with a fall-off to plays about racism, and those awful Nazis who are even better than Nixon to kick around. Progressives are somehow able to make time stand still and make no change at all *happen*; which is something conservatives have been straining to do for ages! (A hard palm to the forehead.)

I don't know how good this Theatre Festival will be. On the one hand, it has enormous conversational and situational ground to mine. On the other hand, good theater with an authentic voice can take a long time to create. Like a major league club, you need a lot of farm teams and a lot of amateur players all over the country who ardently aspire to a dream. You need a lot of Conservative writers, standing on the shoulders of a lot of others to create a zeitgeist which can press on the gas pedal with as much strength as it is now pressing on the brake. And they need to build an audience with a taste for this.

But... it's a start. And it's better than a peck on the head with a sharp progressive rock.

WHAT IF WHAT YOU ARE IS A LOSER?

Artists struggle with this fear constantly. And well, the good news is: it's not all bad.

With losing comes an incredible amount of freedom. Nobody much wants to regulate you, or direct you or to control you – because there isn't much in it for them. And hapless as you are, it would require a *lot* of effort. So you can pretty much say what you want, do what you want, act as you want, dress as you want, dream as you want, do just about anything as you want – as long as you remain unsuccessful. If you consider that most things have very humble beginnings, this places the loser out there on the forefront of just about everything, with the opportunity to create just about anything, and to move the world! I mean, most everything new which ever happened in this world began by mistake. So keep your spirits up first off.

The bad news is that when you are a loser, you're alone. And it's the loneliness which is crushing. No one listens to you. It's extremely difficult to make money. People laugh at you. And without these levers of money and credibility, moving the earth is very difficult. In fact, doing anything is trebly difficult – and this can include just getting out of bed. You may sink into depression as if it were a soft mattress. And you may think, as you stare at the ceiling fan turning in the sultry afternoon air in your cheap, anonymous mildewed room and finish your warm beer, which doesn't taste very good, but it's something, 'Where's the daylight here?' 'Where's the good news?' '

Why not just put the gun in my mouth?' Well, my friend, the daylight is streaming in right in through that window! If only you could open up your heart to feel it, and knock those scales from your eyes to see it.

And. Just to keep my readership up, (Don't jump!), I'm going to suggest something...

Observe those horses racing at the track. The tinier the rider, the faster the horse can go.

So if you're a loser, the first thing you need to do is to face up to it. Then you can find your mount.

Consider the following anecdote...

This anecdote from a Reader's Digest article years ago has always stuck with me. A teacher was writing a letter of recommendation to an Ivy League College for a student of his. After enumerating all of the student's exceptional talents the teacher went on to say, "I can't say he has the qualities of an exceptional leader; but he does make for dependable and resourceful follower." The Dean of Admissions included this note to the teacher with a copy of his Letter of Acceptance. "With all of the natural leaders we admit around here, we can probably use one good follower."

Photos of Troupe Comique by Carl Nelson

We've Had Our Suspicions

CRIMINALS AS SPIRITUAL SAVANTS?

A country song called the *Pittsburgh Stealers* is a "cheatin' song" about a steel mill worker who works the day shift while carrying on with a southern girl whose husband works the night shift. And they're "stealin' luuve, every chance" they git. Sung by a father/daughter team called the Kendalls, it has always been a favorite of mine, if for nothing other than the opening line: "I found myself in Pittsburgh, working in a steel mill."

I loved this vanity of awakening to find myself in some situation with an amnesiac's gawking grasp of how this came to be... Even better, finding myself in this fine melody (with a whining pedal steel) in Pittsburgh having an illicit affair... sneaking around, meeting again and again on back streets. The sentence, "I found myself in Pittsburgh, working in a steel mill." for all its commonality seemed filled with *awe*. It seemed to heap *awe* on top of the prosaic, the quotidian, the dull, daily, repetitive, common grind of very common people like a dollop of ice cream making an *ala mode* out of what otherwise was a pretty common slice of American pie. And then, serving it up for the higher menu price.

Anyway, while singing along with this song on my way to work – putting a dollop of something better on top of my own very common day – the uncomfortable thought struck me that I had heard sociopaths in prison cells describing their criminal experiences in much the same way... as if the crimes they committed were somehow fate …as if some other agency were responsible for their life and actions, and they had just watched, as if from a dream.

Long ago while enrolled in medical school and learning how to interview a patient, I remember the attending saying, "Listen to the patient. They are telling you what is wrong." And it has struck me throughout life how often people are telling me the simple truth. So perhaps criminals are not lying to excuse their guilt; perhaps their lives really *are* aw(e)ful affairs; and we have the criminal as a spiritual savant.

…huh?

And it came to me how evil – and seductive – this sense of *awe* can be; this sense of connection to something much larger and all-knowing and powerful than ourselves. Can proper religious experience and spirituality be so easily hijacked? It's something we search for in the Arts; and yet which is most often found when we pry the top off our Ids, which is, as Webster's describes it, "the undifferentiated source of the organism's energy…", and let loose all Hell.

Photo of the actress Ruth Tru by Carl Nelson

HOW MUCH JUSTICE CAN YOU AFFORD?

The World as It Is.

Okay. So I'm nearing retirement age and still figuring out how things work. One of the things I'm not going to like about dying is not knowing how the story ends… and then not chatting over coffee afterwards with a smart and insightful companion to sort out how it all fit together. But enough of that.

I was in a bar years ago talking with a new acquaintance who was a bit of a hothead. A fellow next to him jawboned in hoping, I suppose, to be included in the conversation. My acquaintance told him to butt out. This fellow, being insulted and drunk, made a retort. My acquaintance took him by both shoulders and pitched him to where he went sliding across the floor. The bartender jumped the counter in a blink and hustled our drunk out post haste, before anyone had a chance to assemble their thoughts… except for the drunk who was shouting and gesticulating his indignation the whole way and then from the outside.

I was puzzled at the time because I had expected my acquaintance to be the person tossed out.

THE PYRAMID OF RATIONAL THOUGHT AND HOW IT LEADS TO EXTINCTION

I decided at the time thatm of course, it is easier to toss out the loser than the winner, of a fight. But as time has passed I've considered that perhaps the bartender had been hoping to remove this obnoxious patron, and my hothead friend gave this bartender his opportunity.

This principle shows itself in the workplace. Someone does something to you that is absolutely wrong. No question. But before you create a stink, and rally the others to the injustice of your plight, you'd best ask yourself… who does the boss like better? Or rather, who fits in around here better? You may be an exemplary employee, but if you're the Odd Duck – usually it's best to keep your mouth shut, retain your low profile, and proceed to plan B.

This is probably the thinking of a lot of illegal immigrants… and poets, too – if you could knock a practical thought into *their* heads.

Photo by Carl Nelson

SELLING ART

Creativity and Sales

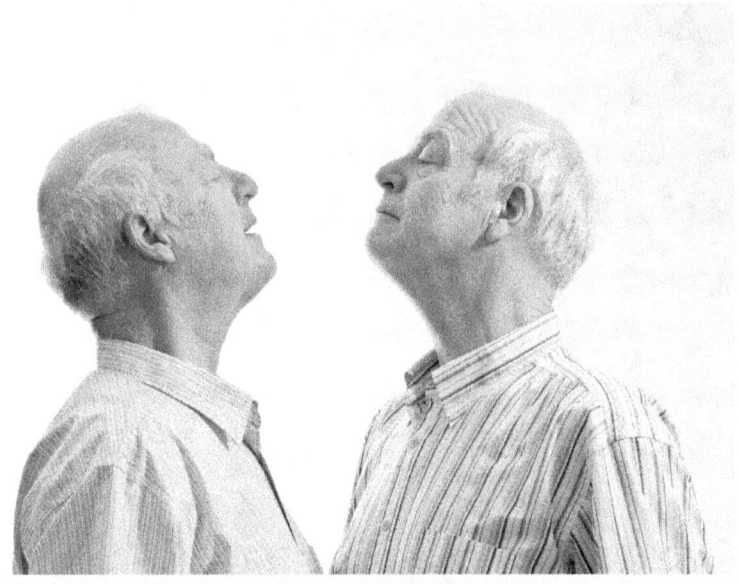

Posture is Everything

SELLING

Selling is a powerful teacher. And one thing selling has taught me is that in order for people to part with their money, they have to feel *certain*. People must feel certain that what you are offering is something they need. And people must feel certain that you can provide what you are offering. After that, you are dickering over cost.

Of course, each of these factors bleed into one another. But what they all have in common is this feeling of *certainty*.

This presents problems for the marketing of art. Because art is full of questionables, imponderables, unnamables, inscrutables, immeasurables, unfathomables, unsociables... the list is long and often tawdry. But all have one thing in common: '*uncertainty*'.

Whether people are buying something or giving money away, they still want this sense of certainty that their assets are not being wasted. So how does one go about selling art?

Well, the only thing more uncertain than art might be people. And traditionally people are sold by dressing them up in certainties. You dress successful; you act successful; you speak successful; you move successful; you associate with success – you appear successful... and you stand your best chance of being purchased successfully, because you have made people most *certain* of your success, and therefore you.

Art is sold in much the same way. What is absolutely undefinable, unfathomable and inscrutable is dressed up in the *certainties*. Let's see how this applies to the theater.

Your average regional theater purchases successful produced plays to present; it uses successful authors; it hires successful directors and actors and set, sound and lighting people. Its productions take place in up to date venues located in the better part of town. It struggles to become the most prominent (successful) theater in town. The more successful the theater appears, the more money it is given. And the more money it has, the less risk it can afford to take. Because, the rule is, you can do anything you want - but you only spend your money with *certainty*.

CREATIVITY

The creative artist creates. They are not re-iterative. They lack production tools, marketing brio... Everything is a prototype. Nothing goes into production. Once something has been produced, then the artist's job is done.

The creative artist tends to spurn the trappings of success because trappings are hindering, because they are already known quantities, because they are *certain*. The artist's job is to pursue what is uncertain, ineffable, unknowable and caste it into the certain. For example, we cannot wholly know a person – but we can write their speech. We can record how they act. We can illuminate and give insight. We can create the feeling of *certainty*. "They feel so real," an observer might say, or even, "I knew that person." Immanence (pagan) or transcendence (Judeo-Christian) are sculpted as certainties. The creative artist sculpts *certainty* from risk. And because money is shy of risk, money necessarily skirts the creative. It is a very great artist indeed who can create the *certain* as a naked thing, and just walk them out of the sea. Even the best, often must dress their creations in some fashionable garb.

So, okay. I'll cut right to the chase and say, yes, money is good for Selling; but it's bad for Creativity. So the next time your hear your local Arts organizations lamenting the fact of there being no money out there for the Arts... just think. Maybe bad for them, but good for us.

Photo by Carl Nelson

DOES ART MAKE YOU A BETTER PERSON?

A lot of people - mostly artists, and especially those whose careers support the arts - say it does. And it's usually only artists – or people who are pitching for a fuller revenue stream – who broach this topic. You rarely hear of a lawyer, or a garbage collector, or a plumber, or a cop, or a mayor, or any of any number of professions raise this question about themselves. They seem to take it for granted that being paid for doing something useful is worthwhile, and hopefully, that participating in life in this capacity makes them a better person. But it may not. That's the way it goes. A person has to get the food on the table.

Because artists have a lot of trouble even 'getting food *to* the table', an alternate reason to justify doing what they are doing would seem necessary. Personally, I would keep looking for a reason, because I haven't seen the theater turning out superior persons. Mostly it makes them like gambling addicts who will squander their last few dollars to create a hit. Their relationships founder; their lawns are not mown; weeds abound in the flower beds, their homes tilt, their porches are gimpy; the children either aren't conceived or grow up a little funny, and financially the whole consortium dances right along the razor's edge.

Actors and writers maintain that assuming the personalities of a variety of characters gives them insight into the human condition. What I've seen is that it adds quite a little arrogance to their own condition. We are always writing/acting ourselves. Who's kidding who? It's as plain as the nose on our faces – which, by the way, haven't changed. Has art made me a better person? I can't say it has. But age and life may have formed me a bit. Just like anyone.

HOW ABOUT BEER?........................

Has beer made me a better person? I can't say it has either. But I enjoy it. And I enjoy art. I enjoy making it. I enjoy watching and listening and experiencing it. I enjoy talking about it. And like most artists, I figure out a method of paying my way. Isn't that enough?

Photo by Carl Nelson of John Ruoff/Mime

Addendum: "There are, of course, more important things than art: life itself, what actually happens to you. This may sound silly, but I have to say it, given what I've heard art-silly people say all my life... Art shouldn't be overrated." – Clement Greenberg, critic

CARNATION HOUSEWIFE EARNS MONEY FROM HOME DIRECTING DRONES FOR THE MILITARY

...Punjab Province, Pakistan...

Margaret DeMarie earned $60,000 dollars last year watching TV!

Editor's Note: You've noticed, if you follow the content of this blog, that we are concerned with the difficulty artists have in supporting themselves financially. So, from time to time, when we run across what seems like a good way to pick up some quick scratch – we try to mention it here on SchnOOdles Blog.

When Margaret DeMarie fell asleep watching the late show two years ago, she awoke to see a job opportunity staring her in the face.

"There it was," she says, "just sitting there floating on the empty screen; an 800 number with the words, 'EARN MONEY FROM HOME'. It was eerie. I felt as if God had spoken. So I called."

"To make a long story short, it involved watching TV for money! And I could do it while ironing, cooking, or even watching my own children. They didn't care. Or maybe they didn't know. But what mattered was whether I had an eye for anything 'suspicious'. When something caught my eye, (and we were trained a bit with a special video as to what to look for) I was to hone in on it by enlarging the screen. (We were shipped a special 'flipper'.) And if it panned out, to pin-point the coordinates and hit 'send' on the special black flipper. I was told a military contractor then analyzed it to forward what they found, if it was 'so warranted', for 'engagement'. I make more or less money depending upon the strategic value of the intel I have forwarded. So I'm directly assisting the war effort and fighting terrorists."

"At first I wasn't making more than a couple dollars a week. But then, the second month in, I happened onto what they call a 'hot target'. And this last month I bought *a dishwasher* with what I was paid! It was installed during the day, so it was a week or so before my husband, Phil, even noticed. Ha!"

"Isn't this a *new dishwasher*?" Phil asked one evening.

I nodded.

"How did we get the money to buy that?"

"Foreign investments, dear," I told him. "I cashed in some foreign investments."

Photo is of a professional model, taken by Carl Nelson

LIVING LONGER

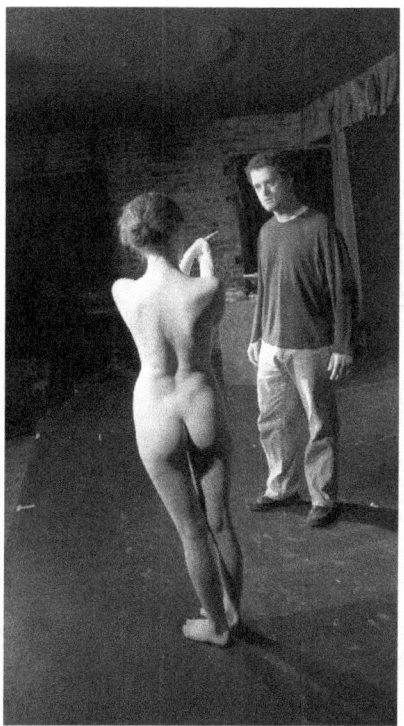

Honey, it's your diet..

It surprises me that some news does not get more of a 'rise' than it does. For example, many years ago I read a small squib in the newspaper which noted that sociologists had found that children of practicing nudists had negligible rates of juvenile delinquency. (Why?) I've never heard anything more about this. And currently our teenage son is behaving well, so we've had no reason to disrobe.

Now, just the other day, in an NPR interview I heard that scientists doing an experiment found that rats fed every other day lived 65% longer than rats fed every day. They also noted that after correcting for other variables, Mormons are suspected of living longer because of the monthly fasting required by their faith.

Well now, if I were to live 65% longer, that would pencil me out at about 150 years, and I would be able to see what is going on around 2100 AD. Moreover, I reasoned, if fasting would enable a person to live 65% longer – wouldn't he/she also necessarily be 65% healthier. *And* if I live well into the advent of The Great Singularity, isn't it possible that I could go on to live forever?

So I've decided to fast one day/week. Yesterday went fairly well. The first few hours following breakfast, I was more ravenous than at any other time. All I could think about was food. And I became appalled at how eating seemed to mark all the most pleasurable landmarks of my day. But I reassured myself that this was surely all my dog and cat and the cows in the field I drove by every morning thought about, so it was a reasonable experience for an animal to have. And it didn't mean I lived a shallow life. Which calmed me.

Then, as the day passed, my hunger took a back seat to other activities. By the next morning, I honestly felt no hungrier than on any other morning. Physically I felt *better*, except for a little listlessness. I was reminded of an observation a friend of mine who served food in a homeless shelter made. He said the men initially were quite docile and happy to find a warm place to eat. But as soon as the food got in them, they could become quite bellicose. All of the anger and resentment they were stewed in began to express itself.

I just became a bit more animated.

Anyway, if this works, you should be hearing quite a bit more from me. At least, time will be on my side.

Photo by Carl Nelson

CARNATION HOMEOWNER LANDS THE GARDENING EQUIVALENT OF A GREAT WHITE SHARK

Sunday, May 6, 2012: Just outside Carnation, Washington, a bedroom community 30 miles east of Seattle, Washington today, a man working in his yard landed what in gardening circles is said to be the equivalent of a Great White Shark. The man, working alone, said he had intended to just cut the runners of the large blackberry vine as he had been doing so for ten years. "But there was something about the sunny afternoon, and the fact that I had worn some heavy jeans that made me just want to go for the gusto," he said later. Getting hold of the roots was just the beginning. "For a while there it had me by both feet and was cutting into my forearms with its spiny thorns. It was a toss-up as to who was going to get the take-down," he said later while posing for this photo. "My wife came out and said, 'Oh honey, you're bleeding!' But at the time I didn't notice a thing." The man said that he would donate the proceeds from the sale of his trophy vine to charity.

Photo by Thawit Nelson

THE NEW AMERICAN ECONOMY

On a recent trip to Florida for a wedding, I may have gotten a preview of our coming American life. Changing demographics and current economic forecasting predict that we're due to have a bumper crop of aging, underfinanced citizens facing retirement soon. These past couple years of economic woes appear to have tossed a lot of them out of their employment sooner than expected. And it looks like, from my brief visit to the snowbird South, that a lot of senior citizens have decided to move to Florida as planned. But rather than relaxing on the beach, they find that to make ends meet, they must find work in the service industries. What does this look like?

Well, just about everyone who worked in the hotel we stayed at looked to be either middle-aged or over 60. The bartender looked like he came of age in the 70s with Steely Dan and Credence Clearwater. The group of men fixing some plumbing and wiring in the wall could have been old Shriners. The waiters we suspected of being on a work-release for older cons. Tattoos and shaved heads and Van Dykes and on the whole, pretty grumpy personalities predominated. Dropping a plate didn't make our waiter miss a beat. He just kept walking.

We generally got one shot at claiming our waiters attention. The maintenance people impressed like a squad of retired cops with large guts and veined legs. And the waitresses were not a good advertisement for a sunny breakfast. I got the feeling that these were people for whom life had not gone as they'd planned.

When we arrived it was dark and my wife couldn't see much out the windows. So she asked the taxi driver if "you have palm trees here?" "That's a stupid question," he replied.

The bus driver wouldn't tell our group we were headed the wrong direction. It was the drunk in the aisle who spoke up. And the guy down the street mowing the sidewalk strip had to catch his breath before responding.

Maybe they were just a brusque variety of East Coast People. Or maybe they were just old and tired.

Or maybe they are both.

Photo by Carl Nelson

NOTED LOCAL FASHION PHOTOGRAPHER IS SWITCHING TO

INSECTS!

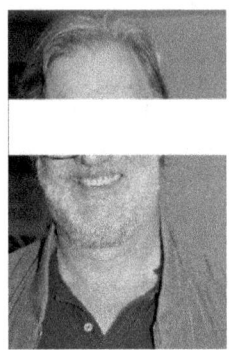

REGULAR MODELS AND ACTORS ARE GETTING TO BE A "PAIN IN THE ASS", HE SAYS.

Editor: The Seattle Fashion Community is all abuzz after the recent declaration by one of its leading photographers that he now intends to use insects and 'bugs' to replace human models and actors in his upcoming fashion shoots. "Your average person knows that he or she can never hope to equal what a professional photographer can do with props, professional staging/make-up/lighting… and what we can't do, we accomplish with Photoshop. Your average person is not made to feel better by looking at all these ads. Quite the opposite! We as professionals dedicate our days to making your average person feel like a failure, like they can never measure up. So, in part, it has a moral dimension," he told The Seattle Celebrity News! during a recent interview. "Plus they work for crumbs," he added.

Read on to hear more:

Seattle Celebrity News! (SCN!): *So you feel that insects more clearly objectify
our present human state?*

Noted Local Fashion Photographer (NLFP): That's right. They *are*
the 99.999999999999999%

SCN!: *Aren't insects hard to work with?*

NLFP: I've never had one talk back or refuse a task. You treat them
right and they'll literally walk the extra meter for you. And they don't
mind sharing a little of the rewards with the other workers in the
industry. Why, just as an example, we used a fairly non-descript, kind
of an everyman bug for a series of motivational posters I was creating
for a large hedge fund which operates out of Brussels. Now this bug,
I'll call him "Bob", lost one of his rear legs partway through the
shoot. Did he call Labor and Industries? Was his agent and/or
lawyer there and on my back in a nanosecond? No. He didn't make
a peep. It was Continuity who picked up on it! Bob said he had five
more good legs, and that the other would grow back in time
anyways. Can you believe that?

We wrapped that puppy without any further disruption. The client
was very happy with the result. Bugs have that 'can-do', hive
mentality which the clients appreciate. They can't tell you what it is,
but I see it in the lens every day. It's the authenticity. 'Bob' is one of
those guys who walks the walk. But there are millions of others.

SCN!: *What about modeling clothes, and such?*

NLFP: Well, they've got 6 legs or more you know! That's a lot of
leg and a lot of shoes. Antennae are great to hang accessories on.
And for some reason those Ladybugs just LOVE the little handbags.
Of course, the camera loves them.

SCN!: *Where do you find your talent?*

NLFP: More often than not they just wander in off the lot, or the
sidewalk. You wouldn't believe the amount of real talent out there.

Of course, there's always the stars. The ones who have that certain something.

SCN!: *Could you give us some hints about some up-and-comers?*

NLFP: Well, there's this almost transparent green aphid who is really causing some buzz amongst the lighting people. And then there's my personal favorite: this Ladybug I'll call Emily. But that's as far as I want to go at this time.

SCN!: *Well. Might we talk to you again?*

NLFP: Sure. Drop by in 3 or 4 months and I think you'll be amazed.

SCN!: *I'll bring my macro lens.*

NLFP: Good choice.

Discouragement: Bob Sees Himself in the Bottom of a Glass

Success Secret #4: Don't Drink and Strive

While we were there, we noticed the talent doing pro bono work.

SCN! photos by Carl Nelson

"ARTISTIC FAILURE IN AMERICA"

I take this title from a blog of the same name. Here's a post to get you started: http://www.artisticfailure.com/category/artists-who-fall-through-the-cracks/

I especially enjoyed some other articles on this blog about "grizzled artists".

What happens to artists as they get older?

By far the largest percentage of artists are financially unsuccessful. (Can you holler, "We are the 99.999999…%!") In a society moving so quickly that it's hindering to stop and puzzle over anything, artists can be slow off the mark. Artistic endeavor tends to be quite introverted. Couple that with failure – or just an initial 'failure to launch' – and you have the recipe for a mesmerizing dance which can pull an artistic mind downward, occupying its thoughts for years. Or, you become successful! for whatever reason, and go on some crazy, lunatic's getaway for your fifteen minutes with the Bitch Goddess.

Is it better to rush headlong? Or stay awhile, look around, get creative, and maybe think your way out of this?

Failure and success are both mysteries. Artists who worship
mysteries often find themselves caught like clouds of gnats buzzing
around these glittering imponderables... and wondering, if they
should continue on - if they can go on -or just fall out of the air?

Or while at the bar with another cold one, 'this all made sense, when
I dreamed it.'

Photo by Carl Nelson

The Camera Follows a Thai Boy on a River Ferry

CINEMA: WHERE QUIET SHOWS ITS MUSCLE

Some years ago I attended a retirement party for a friend of ours where I was seated around a large round table. Partway through the proceedings, I happened to think of something and made a joke of it to the woman sitting next to me. It got a small laugh. What was remarkable was that within the next few moments, the fellow directly across from me (who was a loud and hale sales type) repeated the same witticism to reap loud and generous laughter all around. Then he cast me a look. I don't know whether it was because he was curious as to why I didn't laugh at 'his' joke; or because he had just snitched mine. But it taught me a lesson.

For most of the years I wrote for the theater one question most bothered me. Why did the same people who claimed the stage in life, also have to to claim the stage in theater. I struggled to find a way to write about people and situations which weren't always dominant. What was the point, I thought, in allowing the same characters who dominate us in society to dominate us all over again in the footlights?

I studied sales. I sold. I studied plays. I wrote plays. I studied actors, and I tried a little acting... I even toyed with the notion of starting my own troupe called, The Quiet Theater, whose purpose would be to promote the quiet moment onstage. I imagined holding festivals and giving our prizes for creating the longest, successfully sustained quiet moments onstage. I kept at this for quite some time – not because I had any success – but because I couldn't think of anywhere else to turn. Until finally I'd decided that the role of art is to celebrate life, and like it or not, this was life as the theater celebrated it.

Then I decided to try my hand at directing short films and almost immediately realized the opportunity to depict quiet. Because, in film, the audience's attention is placed wherever the director chooses to place it. And, if the director should choose to ignore the loud fellow stage front... or across the table... Well, that loud fellow can bellow all he wants but the audience is going to watch whatever the camera has been directed to follow. And they will hear whatever the audio speakers most want them to hear. Whether, or not, the film will proceed to hold their attention is another problem. But it occurred to me that cinema is where the quiet finally shows its muscle. And perhaps in this frenetic, sales-driven age, this accounts a bit for cinemas increasing popularity at a time when the theater is fast losing its audience. We all crave a little quiet – and it's more than heavenly to be entertained by it.

Photo by Carl Nelson

Listen up!

LOOK AT THAT SPACE ABOVE YOUR SOFA!

"Every time your Editor posts a note, the readership drops off. So maybe this bit of advice from a very hot, up and coming young Thai Director of Children's Videos will capture your interest."

One of the reasons found for art is that it makes that space on the wall above our sofa look more interesting. No harm. The reverse of this, however, is that if you do purchase a work of art to hang above your sofa – you do so because you would rather look at that art than at the blank wall.

Which brings me to a criticism of actors I make after directing on several occasions for the local stage. Contemporary actors often seem to feel that if their acting embodies their character, then they have done their job. But consider this for a minute in light of what

I've said above. The wall above your sofa perfectly embodies a wall. A brick embodies a brick; a stone a stone… The list, of course, is infinite. Everybody you will pass on the street downtown perfectly embodies themselves. Is everybody on the street interesting? Would you pay to watch them?

A common feeling in the acting community is that 'since I am good at what I do, I should be paid for it'. The Producer's reply to this demand is, "When you make me money, I will pay you money." But this prevailing attitude among actors is a one reason that so many fairly good shorts and films that get produced locally go nowhere – to the frustration of all involved. The actors all feel they've done their job. The writers feel they've done their job. But by the producers benchmark they have failed.

I think they fail in part because neither the actors nor the writers have recognized that they are in sales. It is not enough to be a character; you have to SELL that character. When you've sold your character, the person in the audience says to themselves, "I'm with THEM." That's a fan, and that's a paying customer.

In most local films, I've seen very few actors who are willing to sell. And when there is one who does, the character is often so peripheral that there is no place for the audience to follow them to. This common artistic mentality on the part of local actors seems to be the same with failed salespersons everywhere: " I showed up. I worked hard. I presented the product very professionally and credibly to lots of people." These hopeful 'salespeople' never realize that they weren't selling; they were having conversations; they were visiting. Selling is making people act. Selling is making people want to *do* something. Selling is *wanting* and *asking* and *closing*. So is acting.

Taking Out Insurance on Modernism in Bangkok

MODERNISM CHEWS UP THE THIRD WORLD

"Arguably the most paradigmatic motive of modernism is the rejection of **tradition** *and its reprise, incorporation, rewriting, recapitulation, revision and parody in new forms."* – *Wikipedia*

Imagine Modernism and you might be hard pressed to think of a cultural movement that might more seduce the young ego. Place Modernism in the mix with "scrumptious" Capitalism (as it was described in a Thai film I saw recently while visiting) and you have a cultural buzz saw. I am not a widely travelled person, but just from the information I see and from a recent visit to Thailand this couldn't seem to be more apparent. The young people may still live in Thailand, but on their cell phones and computers they travel about and live in the virtual world with as much familiarity as the mega-rich... even in the orphanage. T shirt slogans capture attention world-wide. And religion, national boundaries, national identities, language, customs... are all looking to be outflanked like the Maginot Line. It's really a bubbling caldron out here in the world. Not necessarily violent, but certainly volatile.

Pray with me.

SCHN00DLE'S BLOG NOW OFFERS THAI FOOD

Our New Thai Cook

Our Editor and Wife have recently returned from Thailand with a Thai Cook, who is now installed at the headquarters of Schn00dle's Blog in Western Washington. Recent breakfast menu was Phad Thai, Green Curry, Fried Rice, Coffee and Orange Juice. When asked about the quality of food he produced, the Cook was quoted as saying, "Yum, yum! Very good!!!" Our whole staff here is very excited.

Photo by Carl Nelson

HOW TO MAKE A LIVING

… as an Artiste'

While waiting to rehearse at a friend's home many years ago, I spied a title on the spine of a thick book in his bookcase across from the dining room table. I thought it read, "Foundations of Paradise". Thinking that this sounds like the title of a great novel I must somehow have missed the existence of, I walked across the room to examine it and found that the title actually was, "Fundamentals of Parasitology". Well! I examined the book anyway and over the ensuing years I haven't found any other book that has come as close – to my thinking – in describing life.

One of the astounding things this book had to say was that **the vast majority of life is parasitical**. They made the point that if you were to completely dissolve most host animals – you would still be able to describe that animal just from arrangement of the remaining parasites.

What does this have to do with earning a living? Well! (I knew you'd ask.) If you were to completely dissolve the physical structure of

most business, you could probably easily tell what sort of business it
was just by the arrangement and type of employees left there
arranged in its airy hive. That is, its parasites. For example, "Oh
look! There are the cooks, and waiters… receptionist… valet
attendants… dishwashers… managers…" My point being, that
where as we see ourselves as an entrepreneurial culture, what
we *mostly* are is a culture of quite successful parasites. For example,
take Bill Gates. What really made his initial fortune was in attaching
himself to the cash stream of IBM by licensing them his software.
Think of the high earning people you know. Do they really make
that money themselves, or are they attached to something (a healthy
money creating firm) via a profitably negotiated agreement which
actually generates their salary?

A second point I gathered from reading this book was that, whereas
most parasites are hard working (in their own way) – what mostly
contributed to their success was their positioning. **Parasites
position themselves to be taken advantage of**. The parasite which
infects sheep positions itself inside of an insect which climbs on top
of a blade of grass which the sheep decides to eat. Parasites position
themselves inside of our food, water, and in our air, (maybe next to
us at the office), everyday.

This is a very important point. Because, for example, last night I was
discussing with a fellow artist friend how he might earn just a
thousand dollars a month. He had worked the outlay problem, so
that with just that small amount of extra earned income he would
become self-sufficient, and he could do his work and most of his
financial difficulties would disappear. It was frustrating how we
racked our brains! Because we felt two intelligent healthy
artists *ought* to be able to figure a way to make just one thousand
dollars a month from their work… from their talent!

It occurs to me now, that we were characterizing the problem from
the wrong position. It is the host which is the expert in earning the
money. **Most companies which make large amounts of money
are able to do so because they have evolved to do so and are
well positioned to appeal to large numbers of customers.**

That's what makes them a host creature. They are highly evolved experts at making revenue.

So, my friend and I were working the problem from the wrong point. **Our real problem is not how to earn money. That's the host's problem. A good host is an expert in how to make the money.** *Our* **problem is how to position ourselves so as to be taken advantage of by the host.** How we should have been putting our minds to work was in looking for a good host.

What's a good host? Well, some entity which makes a lot of money, and which does the sort of thing you'd like to do would be a good first choice! Next, position yourself nearby as possible – and try to look vulnerable and useful and to become indispensible. That is hard-working, reliable, talented, smart, great attitude, friendly, resourceful… and most importantly, available. "Most of being successful is just showing up," as Woody Allen says.

A lot of artists get their back up at this suggestion, especially feminist artists. They stubbornly resist any attempts to take advantage of them. *It becomes a big moral quandary involving the sanctity of their souls!* I think this is wrong headed. They should think more like Bob Dylan who said he'd "snuck in while the door was open – and now they can't get rid of me."

Photo by Carl Nelson (model is John Ruoff)

WE'RE ALL CRAZY!!!

And Finding Friends Where We Can

"The first thing you need to know," a prominent and widely respected psychiatrist I read wrote, "is that we're all nuts". I can't remember his name, but the statement was so outrageous and I liked the notion so much, that it has stuck in my mind ever since. It takes a lot of the pressure off, when you think about it.

And it properly places all those 'realists'.

You want something real, Mr. Hard-headed Realist? Pick up a rock. It will conform to all the laws of physics. It will not disappear nor morph into something new, or suddenly rise out of sight. Nothing unexpected will happen. And my guess is that like reality, it doesn't even know we're here. And like reality – my second guess is – *it doesn't even know it's here*. The only way in which that rock is not appealing to a realist, it would seem, is that lots of 'realists' don't worship it. Which is puzzling to me, because it's a lot easier to find a rock – than to find reality.

It is fashionable currently to genuflect before the glories of the Scientific Mind and to scorn the 'Idiocy of Religion' and all their in-house crazies who currently are held to be fanning all the problems of our Shrinking World. But how do we know what's crazy? What makes doing or thinking one thing more, or less, crazy than doing or thinking another? Most of us take our cue from Christ, "By their fruits you will know them." We generally say someone is acting or thinking 'crazy' if they are doing or saying something which doesn't provide a good outcome. So, the Scientist retreats to his/her laboratory to perform all of these 'crazy' experiments… until the outcome of what he/she has discovered is found to be very successful at explaining what was heretofore a mystery. Aha! He or she was never crazy at all! All along he or she were employing the Scientific Method. But, likewise, the Religious Figure, retreats into the cloisters of his or her faith to perform all of these crazy rituals and to perpetuate the teaching of all of these preposterous ideas… until the outcome is to have spawned an enormously successful society; a society which by nearly all human measure far outstrips whatever had previously come before. Aha! So why does it not seem also that they were not crazy after all but were employing the 'Religious Method'? Like I tell my scientifically biased – and rather rude friends: "If the cult of the EverReady Bunny ever creates another Western Civilization – you can believe I will take it very seriously also."

You wonder why people join cults? You wonder why people lose their lives fighting over the most inane notions? You wonder why people run off into the desert after some charismatic figure? It's very simple: We're all crazy! That's what separates us from the rocks!!! If you're wondering why the populace will follow crazy people, it's because *crazy is the energy we run on*. That's my take. And the more crazy energy you have, the more followers you may get.

This is certainly true of the stage. When directing actors, one of the things a mediocre actor often doesn't understand is that merely 'becoming that character' isn't giving us a great deal. "Congratulations," I feel like saying, "you've become a rock. You're

right up there on the same level as a piece of furniture on the set.
You will be just as interesting as the playwright has written you… but
no more."

If you want to give a memorable performance as an actor, you have
to infuse that character with life. Life is not a rock. Life is not a
chair. Life is not even a desire with dialogue, though we're getting
closer. **Life is an inspired situation.** You have to bring to that
character some of your own 'craziness'. That's how we'll know
you're human… and give you our estimate.

☐ Photo *and* Opinion by Carl Nelson

DALE

Over thirty years ago I worked for a moving outfit where my endless days were spent loading or unloading furniture vans at one of the many loading docks. One of my fellow workers, Dale, was a huge Italian who grew up in Hell's Kitchen. He would skip on his toes across the warehouse floor, much like one of those dancing hippos in Disney's Fantasia. And flicking jabs, while he went from here to there collecting bits of stray string or torn sections of cardboard in order to appear busy. He was tall and powerfully built with olive-skin, oily black hair, large fleshy features and an enormous watermelon of a beer belly which caused him to lean backwards while skipping forwards. He was a former 'deep-water sailor' who harbored in Belltown and drank with his cronies at the Two Bells. His retired pals spent their days keeping track of the whores on First Avenue with red pins which they moved about a large map of downtown Seattle.

Dale was a binge drinker who now and then just wouldn't show up to work. But when Dale was there, if he were in a talkative mood, he'd share with us the wisdom of a merchant seaman. It was generally always the same wisdom: "The question is," he would say with a chuckle as he lifted his meaty forefinger to make his point: "are you da fucker, orderda da fuckee?"

One boring winter afternoon I asked Dale how his Christmas had gone. He had been looking forward to spending the holiday with a woman and her young son in a cheap motel room along Aurora Avenue north. I assumed she was probably a hooker on her day off. "Not so good," he said. "We got in an argument and I ended up throwing the tree and the turkey out the back door." In retrospect, the dark humor of it seemed to be its saving grace. Dale laughed ruefully. But I had the feeling Dale was perplexed, and more profoundly depressed than he could admit. There was something in the nuance of a relationship which seemed to trip him up.

Nevertheless, we seemed to bond in our admiration of the dark humor of it – of those fragile Christmas tree ornaments hitting the asphalt with a *pop!* as the child watched. It was the kind of fantastical horror we might have imagined the Creator to have designed Himself, in a dark moment.

A CHRISTMAS STORY

Just about forty years ago my college career snapped to a close, rather like a rubber band resuming its shape.   And my dream, if I could have described it, was to live in a small studio on the edge of town – out on the prairie – where I would live and paint. Just make paintings, I had no idea of what.

My high school had what was called a Dutch Uncle Program. As a senior, you could pick what sort of career you hoped to have, and they would match you as best they could with someone in the community who did that. You spent the day with them. I had never considered what I wanted to be. I was completely overwhelmed just trying to placate the various factions who competed to run me. The overwhelming narrative of the present (and past, I suppose) had me absolutely pre-occupied.

When I heard the news though about our Dutch Uncle program, a voice rang out clear in my head and it said, "I want to be a writer." This was odd because I had never heard a voice in my head before, and I had never considered becoming a writer. But I wrote that down and handed it to the teacher.

I had read Hemingway in class and was very taken with his simple, poetic way of expressing himself. And across from our lake cabin, where we spent a large portion of our summers, lived a fellow who it was rumored had retired from being a big game hunter in Africa. So, in my mind I conflated the two and pictured spending a day in a writer's bungalow talking (and maybe even drinking a bit) with a guy who looked like Papa Hemingway and had *large* animal heads and trophies hanging around his walls.

What I got was a tired, pasty complexioned, middle-aged reporter in a black suit, tie and shoes behind an office door with guilt letters on a wavy glass pane who wrote the obituaries and military news for the Spokane Daily Chronicle. I, and another student from across town, met with him. I tried to ask intelligent questions, and in return he wrote an assessment for the school councilor that said he believed I could achieve a career as a reporter. This marked the start of the two worlds I tried to live in.

I didn't start writing. I didn't really consider it. Instead, I went to the local state university seventy miles south of town, because everybody in our family went to college there.

There would be a point I imagined when the pressures of the competing factions would abate, maybe just retract a bit, and a 'window of opportunity' would appear just long enough for me to escape. Unfortunately I was either too dutiful a student, or too good at undergraduate work, and I got into medical school.

So there I was lifting the body flaps off cadavers and interviewing patients, trying to understand people as only a writer would - patients who just wanted to get well. I was long on conversation, short on treatment. I joke, when people say, "what a waste of an education" –

that I have probably saved more lives by quitting medicine than a lot of doctors have by continuing.

So, I'm adrift from medicine and set on becoming an artist. This is about 35 years ago.

It was soon apparent after the student support stopped, that I was going to have to work *all the time*, just to eat and keep a roof over my head.

I decided I needed to lower and stabilize my living costs. So I bought a home.

My top price was fifteen thousand. And I found a repossessed, fixer-upper, in the poorer southeast end of Seattle. Say whatever you want about minorities, but they keep the rents down. And this place was packed with everybody.

The Southeast Asians in the neighborhood would squat sucking cigarettes at the bus stop. My neighbor two houses down, friendly Hwang, worked as a cook downtown. Hwang and I discussed making his garage into another bedroom for his innumerable relations.

Kiddy-corner across the street was a quiet, comely single black mom with a shy young son; a woman who seemed – quite beyond anything she did – to attract black males in abundance: normals, Superflys, the gamut... And, of course, there would be the dust-ups. Early one morning (around 3 am) I remember waking up to the sound of pouring rain and some fellow yelling his head off. I rolled over and remembered muttering, "I wish someone would shoot that Son-of-a-Bitch!" "Pop! Pop! Pop!" That was the last I heard. The rain continued.

Anyway, I succeeded in lowering my living costs to house payments of around $103/month. And my studio was as big as the numbers of walls I decided to knock out. I hadn't anything to steal. And I'm big enough I generally wasn't bothered. I purchased and installed a wood stove, and one side of the equation was solved.

I also wanted to make a living as an artist. It didn't need to be grand, but I wanted that sense of moving forward and relishing each day. (Forget marriage and having kids.) Drawing portraits seemed like it would fill the bill. I'd watched others seemingly make a living at it. Flattery and narcissism have brought artists paying customers down through the ages. I studied figure drawing twice weekly, including the face. I thought I could bring something to it, as they say.

So to get my feet wet I started off at the beach at Alki Beach where there were not many customers and it was illegal. So I was run out of there fairly quickly. The Seattle Center required all sorts of bureaucratic rigmarole. The downtown waterfront looked ideal, what with the continual flow of tourists, but that area had been homesteaded long before I got there. I considered paying the meter and setting up shop in a parking stall just under the viaduct, or better yet, right along Elliot Avenue, the thoroughfare along the boardwalk. Then I had the grand idea of going into business with Ivar. He was our local restaurateur legend. In all the ads he was very homespun and friendly. He had run with the local art legends. There is a statue of him now on the downtown waterfront feeding a bronze seagull. Part of his building along the street was unused at the time.

Ivar wasn't big on the idea. He had plans to add on. It seemed to me that live portrait art done in a front section of his business would be just the thing to attract the tourist crowds and "add a bit of artistic elan to the enterprise!" But when I pressed him on it, Ivar said, "What do you think? I'm lying to you?" And ran me off.

So I ended up at the Market. The Pike Street Farmers Market is where a lot of artisans in Seattle traded. For $3.50/day I could rent about 4 feet of counter space to show off my wares to a seemingly endless flow of people. It was outdoors and cramped, but it had the crowds. And it was romantic. You showed up early, around 7am, while they were shoveling crushed ice at the fish stalls because that was when the stall placements were made. Then you'd set up, and maybe go in for coffee at either Lowells or the Athenian (plus breakfast, if you were making money) until the shoppers arrived.

The bar was already open and the alcoholics at the counter already past their first drink of the day. One of my friends there noted how, when the alcoholics arranged themselves before their first drink of the day, they would use a bar towel draped across their neck so that with one hand they could guide their other shaky hand with drink to their mouths so as not to spill. After the days work, we'd put our stuff away and have a beer there ourselves. (Again, if we'd made any money.)

Unfortunately, I *wasn't* making any money to speak of, and as November arrived it was getting damned cold. I dressed warmer. I stood on cardboard. I cut the ends off my mitten fingers. But I was getting bored with standing in the cold. When you're not making any money, and freezing, there really isn't a lot to say. You're not in the mood to talk. You're glum. I started looking around. A bright spot was the playing of the metal kettle drums. That particular metallic banging for money carried down the Market concourse and out into the street – then echo its return until the cold air was a scintillating jumble of hovering notes, a romantic world-sound. The days, at times, never seem as beautiful as when you were poor.

But I needed more money. So I made my way uptown to the department stores. Somehow or other I found myself in the office of the manager of the Bon Marche (now Macys). I showed him my portraits and pitched him.

When I think of a lot of the people I've liked, a large percentage of them are businessmen. They tend to be honest and decent. They're tough, but then it's very hard to be decent in this world without being tough. Anyway, I liked this fellow. And I think he liked me, for some reason. We agreed on a percentage and hours and he took me to a spot in the lamp department at the head of the escalator on the 5th floor, which he thought would do. (Later, they even made up some posters for publicity.)

I commented on the way up the escalators that it had never made sense to me why we had to walk all the way around to continue our climb to the next floor? Mr. Smith (that may have been his name) said that was because it gave them a chance to show off their

merchandise on each floor as the customer walked past. As we
descended he added, "And we know exactly how long it takes for a
customer to descend the escalator, and what he can see of the floor
below during each second of his descent." I found this very
interesting. As I sat in my artist's chair day after day watching the
activity around me, it was apparent that a department store is not the
still display of wares the occasional visitor might think it to be. No.
"If merchandise does not start moving within the first half hour that
it is placed out there, it is either moved or replaced," Mr. Smith said.
And I witnessed this, as I sat there through the Christmas rush.

I wasn't doing that great a trade – yet the manager never threatened
to can me. "How's it going?" He'd say on one of his passes through
the store. "I don't know," I said despondently one day. "I think I
could take off all my clothes and I still couldn't get their attention."

"Well. Don't do that," he admonished.

No matter where you are in this life, if you just sit still, you'll notice a
lot. If you sit in a department store, you'll see how mobile all of the
merchandise is – as I've said. If you sit at the head of an escalator,
you'll get an idea of how dangerous they can be. They would eat
shoes, rubbers. Childrens' small fingers and mittens could get caught
in the moving handrail, where it curved at the top of escalator to
return. There was an emergency button placed there to stop the
escalator for a reason. An older wizened Jewish woman ran the lamp
department with a younger middle-aged daughter who looked to me
like a gypsy. I was commissioned to do her portrait. But I don't
think they must have particularly liked it, as I don't remember them
saying anything. I couldn't decide if the mother were trying to line
me up with her or not. On the whole, I think not. She was too
canny to want to introduce her daughter to a portrait artist.

But it wasn't like I sat still and waited for things to happen. I
changed my display samples. I saw that sensitive pencil drawings just
weren't going to make it. I saw that what sold were things with
'punch'. So I upgraded to charcoal. And line-shading was risky, as
much as I loved it. It was hard to do correctly. Also, a public
portrait artist has quite a bit of surface to cover in 20 minutes. The

bigger the better, for pricing. And there is nothing like smudged charcoal to cover that ground. So, much as I detested it, I began smudging my charcoal. Then I discovered that the smudge sticks of rolled paper work like fattened pencils. Sometimes a compromise bends your way. And I added a conte crayon line. I worshipped the drawings of Michelangelo and Da Vinci, and conte seemed as close as I would get to my personal Renaissance.

Still, things moved slowly. As I've aged I've realized that some people have charisma and attract a crowd. Some don't. I'm in the latter group. It was said of the famous modern mathematician (Godel) that he was "anti-charismatic". He once voiced the answer – in the midst of a mathematical society meeting – to a conundrum which had eluded mathematicians for 2,000 years. He was ignored. I'm not maintaining that *my* anti-charisma is on that level. But I *would* say that when I speak, people lose interest. Unless it's a quick witticism, by three sentences I pretty much have to step around to block their exit.

I did notice though, that customers are attracted by *other* customers. So I would always try to be busy drawing: from a photo, or, from a face I liked and cajoled into sitting for me.

It seemed to be the rule that whoever had an interesting face, judged themselves unbecoming and a portrait was the last thing they wanted to sit for. And those who judged themselves good-looking were almost invariably uninteresting artistically – you could virtually hear the pencil yawn and the eraser sigh. The years since have taught me that this experience of the ugly duckling seems to permeate all of life.

But to continue. I thought that perhaps my prices were too high. So, I had discount prizes. I would draw a face, smudge it over – and then offer, at *half-price!*, a portrait to whoever could name the famous person that it was. They usually won! Hooray! "You are very clever!" (Have a seat!)

Then, considering some might have a limited budget, I tried selling just the portrait of a nose for 75 cents, or an ear for 50. And I put them in the cute little frames.

(To Be Continued...)

Drawing by Carl Nelson

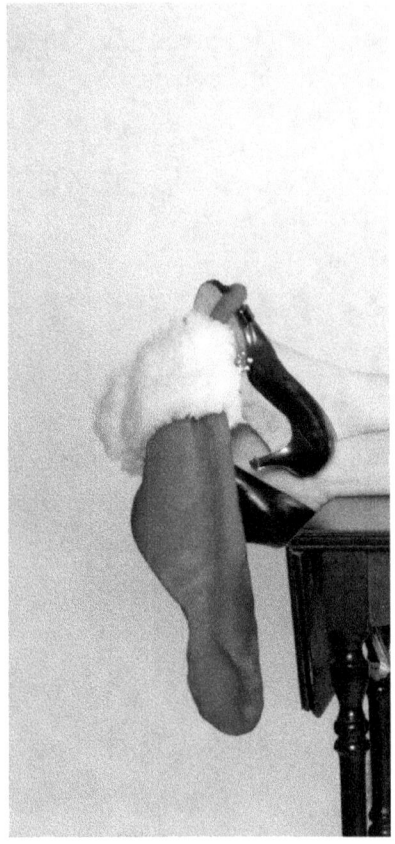

A CHRISTMAS STORY

Part Two:

Still, things remained pretty slack. So I took any sort of work customers offered. As Moliere used to admonish his troupe (to paraphrase a bit), "When the King wants to see a performance you don't tell him you're not ready." I drew from small and poorly lit snapshots. I drew pets. A lady brought me a two inch by two inch poorly lit snapshot of her shaggy dog standing against the wind with its hair being blown backwards across its face. The only identifying features, besides all of the yarn-like hair, were three dots. Two suggested eyes, the other a nose. A magnifying glass got me that far. For the rest of the fifteen dollars I had to invent a lot of dog. But I did it.

And I drew babies. Babies' features are near identical. Their
expressions are fleeting. In fact, everything they do is fleeting.
Especially posing.

The key to neonatal recognition is in accurately recording the
distance between their significant features such as the eyes, the nose-
eyes-mouth triangles, how far off are their ears? Their mother's
brains are built like airport scanners that can pick the terrorist from a
million other faces. "That's not her! That's not my baby. That
doesn't look like my baby!" (Well, don't shout! What part of it do
you think *does*?)

What I'd do for fifteen dollars! One of the first things I did with my
newly made money was to purchase a bigger magnifying glass.

You had to watch the dark humor. *Don't* tell a sweet little girl, "You
move, and I'll punch you." The mother's gasp, just behind me,
sucked all of the air from the room.

Nice things happened. A lot of people left very pleased that you'd
noticed the same special quality about their loved one that they
loved. Some felt you'd done an "honest assessment". And one
thought the chin was too long. (Actually, the nose was too short.)
The best were younger children with dark hair and eyes. You
couldn't miss. And it was fun to observe their silence, or their
chatter. And I didn't worry too much if they moved a bit. Most
humans (and animals too) repeat the same gestures. Patience works.
Which is probably why we invented it. I just had to be sure to finish
in around twenty minutes.

The only exception to this were the pretty young women who would
sit for their portrait, draw you into conversation and then ask, with a
rather demur turn to their voice and a slight quiver to their eyelid:
"Have you ever drawn women nude?" This is the sort of experience
you earn as a portrait artist. It's like your Canadian Club.

Like any young man, most of the women I met were on the job. One
was a psychologist: "I don't think that you can actually produce the
quality of portrait you have on display in the twenty minutes you

have to do them in," she suggested. I didn't argue with her. I also didn't say that anyone who won't cheat or steal a little for their art, probably hasn't the balls to get anywhere. The last conversation I remember having with her, she insisted I was depressed. I told her I didn't think I was depressed; that I was just feeling the way it was. You don't understand she said, "Depression is a very, serious disease."

Well, I would agree with her partly there. Art is a *very, serious disease*. This is probably why parents become so concerned when they detect signs of it in their loved ones. And there was the police officer who I went out with for a drink. "Well," she said, "if it's not working out for you, you can always do something else." You go silent as an artist when you hear that. It's like saying, "Well, if you don't like your cancer, you can kick it."

A thought that slowly dawns on you as an artist is that most of the way you experience the world and/or 'feel' is illegal. In the eyes of normal people, you are not simply describing failure and how it feels – you are suffering from a *very, serious disease* – and/or you're a whiner, loser, complainer… (You go to the Thesaurus yourself. It's too depressing.) If they feel that way about it, you have to wonder why they have to ask? It's hard to skip these failed conversations before you can find out if they are the sort of person with whom you'll have them.

I finally happened upon someone though, who it seemed I connected with. And it happened through the first (and only) blind date I had ever arranged for *myself*. One day I was finishing up a portrait of some …little girl, I imagine. A small crowd had gathered. And as the girl rose to claim her drawing I heard this high pitched squeal from behind: "Oh. Would you draw *me*?!!"

I turned. And there was a pretty tall Miss Piggy, with a huge pink foam head and flannel costume, and, of course, with those long flowing blonde locks and batting eyelashes… lovely round nose. She had me from hello. "Sure," I said. "Sit yourself down."

"Oh goody," she said.

I started on the portrait; made a show of needing a much larger piece of paper. She stayed in character. I imagine we traded in Sesame Street gossip. But as the crowd dissipated and I finished up – we made a date to meet at the base of the escalator when she got off around seven.

I was delighted and surprised to find I'd just made myself a date with a tall, healthy, good-looking, honey-haired blonde who looked a lot like Candice Bergen. As it turned out, she was a highly intelligent, down on her luck professional tennis player who happened to have ended up broke in Seattle after losing one too many matches… and latched onto the first job she could find.

We attended the theater. I believe I cooked dinner for her once. She spent a day visiting with a famous young woman tennis player she'd coached who came to town during the Virginia Slims tournament. (Have I remembered that right? Did a cigarette company actually promote a tennis tournament?) And going broke trying to do something seemed the most natural thing in the world to her. Or, at least, I can't remember talking about it. Anyway, the last I corresponded with her, she had written me a note from the Bahamas where she was coaching at a plush resort. I sent her some ash from the Mount Saint Helens eruption.

And then came the *Christmas Rush*. You get down to those last few days and the shoppers become like desperate fish who will bite on anything. They are literally tossing their money. And my business picked up too!

I've never worked so hard. You have to make hay while the hay is making, and everyone was working hard right up to the line.

By late afternoon, Christmas Eve, I was emotionally exhausted, completely spent. At the drawing group I attended we had a curious Chinese fellow who would check the arrangement of the features of our model with a measuring tape. We'd be drawing away as he pulled the Carpenter's tape out to check on the foreshortening of a limb. Then there would be a "*snap!*" as he got the measurement he wanted and left the tape to recoil. Not many drew like that, thank God.

But I judged the proportions – and everything else – by feel. And by mid-afternoon Christmas Eve I was *totally* numb. My feeling needle had slumped over like Salvador Dali's clocks and expired on the floor. I had no idea what I was doing. I would look out at a face; then look at the easel without any sense of proportion whatsoever. I was moving by rote; winging it on a hope and a prayer; walking the tightrope without a rope. You don't turn down money.

The store was closing as I reached my very last customer. He was a drunk, quite disheveled, pudgy, thirty-something year old male with a very red nose. "I want you to draw my portrait," he slurred. I helped him to sit.

We did the best we could. He said he had been walking around for hours (probably 'round and 'round a bar glass) and just couldn't figure out what to give his parents for Christmas. Then he happened by my display when it hit him! That what they would like would be a portrait of *him*. I nodded, as I drew, as if that were very insightful. But still, for the life of me I couldn't tell what the hell I was doing. And this was taking far too long. So finally, he decided he would give me some help by stepping around the easel.

"The nose is too small," he said.

The standard cynical definition of a portrait is, that it is a painting in which "the nose is too large". (Maybe Whistler said that.) So I gave a rueful laugh.

I worked on, until finally even *he* was becoming restless. "You about done?" He said querulously.

"Just another minute or so," I answered, softly. I kept looking but I just couldn't get a reading on whether or not it was right.

He awoke suddenly, again. "Because I have somewhere to *be*."

In medical school, I was doing an externship in the Harborview ER where I lost a hooked needle in the bloody scalp of a drunk. When you stitch a bloody scalp laceration, you're never supposed to let go of one end of the needle with the clamp, until you have the other end securely clamped. How could I have screwed that up? I had a flashback of the loud, drunken interrogation about what was "*taking so looong? Do you know what the fuck you're doing!*"

I looked around. To my surprise all of the lights in the store had been turned out, and we sat within an oblong of light of the one lamp which illuminated him and the one drawing lamp which illuminated my easel. Just on the edge of the circle of light I heard a 'whimpering'? I squinted further into the darkened perimeter, and there were three Dobermans standing patiently in choke collars backed by their handlers in black leather jackets who were doing a last sweep of the store. "Are you going to be much longer," the most authoritative one of them asked me. (With remarkable deference, I thought at the time.)

"No. I think I'm done right now," I said. I presented the drawing to my 'customer'. He looked it over. Said thank you, relieved, as if however it looked, I had solved a big problem for *him*. He paid me and left. And I packed up and left immediately after.

I rode the #7 home that Christmas Eve with about half a bus load of other non-committal passengers; just a portion of the left-out people of this world, not late for anything or needing to be anywhere. I walked to my house and scooped up some dinner from the crock pot meal I had left simmering all day. I sat in my bare living room in my one overstuffed chair and footstool with my two cats layered on my legs for warmth and watched the many colored lights on my jade plant twinkle. One strand of indoor lights will go 'round and 'round a tiny jade plant till it shone brightly as a burning bush.

Photo by Carl Nelson

Corporate Culture

Part 1:

The Office Rat

THE HIERARCHIES

VERSUS

A LITTLE BIT OF GOD

There's the old joke that life is like pulling a dogsled – if you're not the lead dog all you see are assholes. What does this have to do with Art?

Well, before you can get people to appreciate beauty, first you have to get their attention. And this is not so easy. The problem even

164

perplexed Jesus, who famously griped, (with my paraphrase and
exclamation point) "Heaven is all around us, if only you have the eyes
to see!"

"Well that's all fine and good," most reply, "but I'm a practical
person and I've got to keep my sights on the rear-end of this dog
ahead of me. Go away and don't bother me."

People who have tried to help impoverished artists find that "you
give them money, and they just spend it on more art materials." What
art achieves, at least for the evanescent moment, is to get our eyes off
the rear-end of that sled dog ahead of us. And that's intoxicating.

I'm often frustrated when I find reason useless for my ends. But I'm
not alone in this quandary. Does being an artist sound reasonable?
As artists start to work each day, we all pray, or meditate, or maybe
just mutter a bit, or tie one shoelace backwards for inspiration.
Because a little bit of God can go a long way.

Poster and Photo by Carl Nelson

"THE NEXT GOOD IDEA YOU HAVE MAY BE IRRATIONAL "
(By Sales and Theatre guru, Milton Odwell)

Many large corporations with hundreds of workers who have their headquarters in Seattle wall themselves off from salespeople by offering only one generic phone number, no mention on their website of a staff directory, and a receptionist who, when you call, sends you directly to a 'vendor's voice mail' before you can say, "Hey!"

So what do you do? Especially, if you're a salesperson and know that this company needs your product and/or pricing?

One of the things you can do is to call one of their out-of-state offices. Then you ask whoever answers if they would direct you to the person who handles the purchasing and leasing of the product you offer. They will often tell you that this is *all* handled by their headquarters in Seattle. So you ask them for the person who would handle it "there" – and they often will give you a name. If they don't, then you call another out-of-state office. "Oh, and by the way," you ask, "Do they have a direct phone number?" Often times they will give you that also.

A playwright's mind is often like a large corporation. It is often beset with a very large problem and does not want to be bothered. And so it often walls itself off from considering just those ideas that it needs to perform its mission, by blocking all the ports of entry and interruption. This mindset can get you really stuck.

At readings, common feedback often reinforces these inclinations. Listeners often recommend that the playwright cut this and/or that scene and/or authorial interruption from the script as they bear 'no rational relationship to the narrative line'. This is a great way to never find the story. I support following up on those blips which seem out of context, or wholly divergent from where the story seems to be heading. This is the authorial equivalent of calling Miami. And it has a better chance of success.

SUCCESS

"When the competition is over, the Kings and the Pawns all go back in the same box."
— Italian proverb

From what I've been able to glean from Wikipedia, each fertilized human embryo represents a huge Oklahoma-like Land Rush representing an average *30 million* sperm participants. The man or woman you're looking at in the picture above sleeping under a thin blanket represents the winner of such an event. It's amazing to think that each person you encounter every day has been enormously successful. And I mean on the level of a Bill Gates.

So what about this poor man or woman? Well, my first thought would be that indeed, "winning IS everything". By that I mean, success in one sphere does not necessarily transfer well to another. "That was then, and this is now."

But, in fact, we're all has-beens. It will be the very rare person who can replicate the success they had by just being born. So I think we shouldn't be alarmed so much by failure… By being broke? Well, yes. Maybe a bit – or even a lot! We have to eat. But I think each of us should get up each day and walk with our head up and our shoulders back – in light of the immense success we already are... even if we're a little hungry and sleeping under a bridge.

ABOUT THE AUTHOR

The author lives in Belpre, Ohio where he moseys about. Grinding his axe writing essays seems to keep him from ruining his poetry.

Carl Nelson spent twenty years in the Seattle theater community, during which time he wrote and produced plays, directed others, and performed whenever the talent was missing but a body still needed.

Before that he did stand-up comedy.